My Daught

Natasha Badhwar was born in Ranchi, grew up in Kolkata and refused to accept Delhi as home for the next three decades.

She began her career in broadcast journalism with New Delhi Television (NDTV) as the first female videographer in news television in India. She quit thirteen years later as vice president, training and development. She now works as an independent film-maker, media trainer, columnist and fashion entrepreneur.

Natasha writes the popular column 'My Daughters' Mum' in *Mint Lounge*, and blogs at http://mydaughtersmum.blogspot.in.

She lives in New Delhi with her husband and three daughters.

My Daughters' Mum

Essays

Natasha Badhwar

**SIMON &
SCHUSTER**

London · New York · Sydney · Toronto · New Delhi

A CBS COMPANY

First published in India by Simon & Schuster India, 2017
A CBS company

3 5 7 9 10 8 6 4 2

Simon & Schuster India
818, Indraprakash Building,
21, Barakhamba Road,
New Delhi 110001

www.simonandschuster.co.in

PB ISBN: 978-93-86797-00-1
eBook ISBN: 978-93-86797-01-8

Grateful acknowledgement is made to *Mint Lounge* which publishes the author's column. Portions of this work were also originally published in the following: 'Saying Sorry to Shahrukh Khan' in *Newslaundry*; 'A Manifesto for Working Women' in *Sheroes*; 'To Fail without Feeling Like a Failure' and 'The Happiness Key' in *The Indian Express*; 'Small Doses of Joy' in *Outlook*; 'You Have Forgotten Some Things, Mamma?' in *Femina*; and 'In Praise of the Dehati Aurat' in Asian News International.

Typeset in India by SÜRYA, New Delhi

Printed and bound in India by Replika Press Pvt. Ltd.

MIX
Paper from
responsible sources
FSC® C016779

To my parents
Sudha and Trilok
for letting me fly, so that I could always find my own way home

I wanted to be all of myself at the same time,
so I wrote wrote wrote
myself into fullness.

It Is Okay to Talk About This

I am carrying within me various permissions for myself. Simple words meant to override the messages I had internalized while growing up.

Celebrate your children.

Keep yourself together.

Find the essential truth within your parents.

Make time to cherish yourself.

Protect love, so that love can protect you.

A story that revisits me every day is what happened when I was twelve-and-a-half years old. Our two older daughters—Sahar and Aliza—are fourteen and twelve right now. Our youngest daughter Naseem is nine.

'Are you twelve-and-a-half years old, Sahar?' I asked our firstborn a couple of years ago.

'Yes,' she said.

'Exactly 12.5.'

'Yes.'

I showed her my incision-scar. I have forty-five stitches running down the centre of my right arm. It is shorter than my left arm by four inches. 'I was twelve-and-a-half when this happened,' I said.

She nodded. I have told my children about my fall from the roof of our home when I was a child.

The truth is, I had jumped. At 5 am on a winter morning in January, I had jumped from the fourth floor and crashed on to the concrete ground below. I had decided that it was better to die than face the day.

I had attempted and survived suicide.

~

A child tries to kill herself; a child doesn't die.

The child grows up and has children of her own. Her fears, her guilt, her desire to talk about her suicide attempt—these become a part of the story that haunts her. A story she has to understand.

Memories come back and perch on her shoulder. They take the shape of dreams. They visit as tears.

She wants to talk to her parents. She does not want to hurt them again. She does not want to make them remember. She wants to ask for forgiveness. She wants to cry in her mother's arms. She wants to be loved. Openly. So she can love openly. So she can abandon the fear that she will be punished when she becomes a parent. That history will repeat itself.

It is okay to talk about this. She knows that.

~

My mother Sudha is the fifth daughter and sixth child of her parents. There were eight siblings. Her closest sister committed suicide in her early twenties. Her name was Chanchal. My mother talks to me about her. She speaks of the household they grew up in. She was four years old in 1947 when this country became independent and was partitioned into India and Pakistan. Her mother, my Nani, was expecting her seventh child when the family abandoned their ancestral home in Lahore and moved to Amritsar. It took years, decades, generations, for them to feel at home again.

Like most Indian families, both sides of my parents' family are obsessed, to some degree, with the male child and his privileges. My mother tries to rationalize it. She tells me brutal stories of how other significant adults were mean to girls, but she becomes protective about her own mother and father. They were valiant and fair.

I did not get a chance to know my mother's parents very much, but my Nani appears in my dreams sometimes. I want to speak to her. I want to know how parents can love their daughters and still not give them permission to have any agency over their lives. I want to know how they can silently reaffirm that girls must have no control over their destinies. It angers and baffles me. I know that Nani won't have the answers.

I am determined to break the script my grandmothers lived and died by. They were powerful women who did not have the authority to protect their own children. They were caregivers for everyone but they did not have permission to assert their needs and desires. Ammi, my mother-in-law, would show me the way.

There are those who will celebrate the 'sacrifice' of women; I insist on calling out abuse.

My father's mother had three sons. Dadaji, my father's father, is the only grandparent I really got to know. He lived past ninety. We were both loving and confrontational in our relationship with each other. I defied him in ways that no one else did. We taught each other a lot.

Dadaji took the news of my decision to marry Afzal—a Muslim from Uttar Pradesh—very badly. For a few days, he seemed to lose his grip on reality. He began to hallucinate and became paranoid. We did not know whether he would recover, but he did. When he met my in-laws eventually, he was gracious, soaking in conversations in Urdu with my father-in-law and Afzal. When our youngest child Naseem was born, he called out to her each time we visited, and glowed with happiness when she responded to him.

Raising children and being in love make me vulnerable. I have learnt that vulnerability is not weakness. Recognizing one's vulnerability is pure courage. It gives me the will to stand up to oppression—to be honest, to confront. It makes me see things with clarity.

~

As with most children, my early writing in school tended to focus on my family. When we went through hard times as a household—shifting cities and schools and missing our father as he joined the private sector in the 1980s—I wrote thinly-veiled fiction for my school magazine. I wrote of the death of a sibling. I wrote of longing to belong and be understood.

My words seemed to upset my parents. My mother sat me down next to her, held the school magazine in her hand and asked me what I meant to say in the story I had written. I felt like a culprit. I stopped writing. I became lost and confused. My voice turned small. I lied a lot.

In my early thirties, I began to blog anonymously after our second daughter Aliza was born. Aliza is a liberator. Every time I feel fear—on the dentist's chair or on the doctor's examination bed—I chant *Aliza Aliza Aliza*. She is courage.

I write to express happiness. I have an immense capacity for being happy. I clap my hands and hop, skip and jump. I smile in my selfies. I don't find enough space in the real world to express my joy. I take photos of it, write fragments of poetry and post it online. I go to my children's room and make funny faces. Speak in strange accents.

I write to see myself through the tunnel of darkness. I write myself out of the bottomless well.

I sort out my position and my feelings by writing about them.

I write, also, to make place for love. This is important. We refuse to recognize love, for fear of what it might ask from us. We shoo love away, and destroy it. We express love as anxiety and anger. Let's separate fear from affection. Let our love be seen and felt.

I feel anxious about what is considered 'normal' in most families. The notion of family and community honour horrifies me. The idea that children must be trained—so, they lose their spontaneity and confidence—alarms me. We have a callous attitude towards mental health issues. We tolerate the abuse of our own children because we are too timid to challenge power structures. I write to dismantle hierarchies; I write to honour the child in each of us.

The soul of the child is nourished by the well-being of the parents. I write to banish the silence between my parents and me. It has been my life's journey to cut through the fog of expectations and connect with the essential self of my mother. Unless I recognize the layers within them, I will not be able to understand the layers within me. Perhaps the root of my sorrow is not having a direct connection, a deep intimacy with my mother. And the root of her sorrow is the same.

I write to keep my own head above the water; to remind myself to be gentle and humble; to slow down and make time for each other.

I write to remember my mother's unsung sister and the child who decided to give up too soon. I write to honour the difficult love of parents. I write to speak to my brothers, my husband and children; to let them know me, to build trust again. I write to reclaim my father.

I write at the risk of exposing myself to ridicule, so that the fear of derision falls away as I go along. I write to banish shame.

I want readers to feel that their own stories and personal experiences are important, and sharing doesn't diminish us. We can seek support. We can find a language that connects us. We can recover our strengths—for, each of us is a storehouse of power and healing.

To restore the tattered fabric of the world around us, we must return to nurture its core unit—the family and the individual. I write about friends and co-workers, love and marriage, unexpected encounters and relationships, raising daughters and the idea of India. I write about parenting and self-love, and about learning to fight for the sake of rejuvenation.

I write for you and me and for a gentler, more just world.

My Daughters' Mum

"Dinner first, Naseem," I say. "Ice-cream after dinner."

"I will write in my article," she says, "that Mamma does not let me eat ice-cream."

girl

Smart

You Have Forgotten Some Things, Mamma?

We are the parents of three children, but don't let the number distract you. The more kids there are, the better the photos. The more there are, the more time off a parent gets—and the higher the sense of achievement when anything gets done at all—like being on schedule for the school bus, or noticing that one has forgotten one's phone within ten minutes of leaving home.

Now, you may stop to wonder at the kind of people we are. Fairly unthinking in our actions, you may conclude. Somewhat inspired in our decision-making, but generally quite foolish.

You may be right.

~

What can I say? I had always fantasized about being a parent. I had been making notes in The Parent Project file for over a decade—well before our first child was born. And they were good notes.

The first time I held my baby in my arms, I was still on the delivery table. She was wailing like the just-born infant she was. I began to sing to her. Her cry trailed off. I was sure she was listening. She knew my voice.

It took me a while to realize that my singing wouldn't calm her down each time. Within a fortnight, my husband, my mother and I had a handy checklist to figure out why the baby might be crying. It went like this:

1) Is she hungry?

2) Needs to be burped?

3) Has a wet nappy?

4) Wants to be rocked to sleep?

5) Is her nose blocked?

6) Back to square one.

Sometimes, it was none of the above.

With time, many of my closely held myths and certainties about parenting fell away.

I now know that parenting is not just about creation. Creation comes later. It is about destruction first—the soundless collapse of your ego. Saying goodbye to the self that you were before the first pregnancy. Redefining an identity.

Being a parent means feeling, at once, a sense of pride and a sense of loss. It's hard to put your finger on what is missing. You sift through childhood memories again and again for clues—for a sense of what has been mislaid. You sift through them, also, to identify fears that you don't want to pass on and the trauma you don't want your kids to relive.

I soon realized how easy it had been to proclaim I'd be unlike my parents and how complicated it was to be independent of my sociocultural baggage.

In the middle of my life, when I embarked on a parenting trip, I didn't mean to sign up for a self-improvement course. I had things to teach, not learn. I knew my moral science lessons by heart. I knew manners and etiquette. I knew the websites to look up, and had a hardback book with pictures for ready reference.

Yet, suddenly, the things I thought I understood didn't seem all that effective. They asked to be tested and engaged with constantly. Should adults necessarily be obeyed? Are teachers always right? How much ice cream is too much ice cream? Can one wear crocs with a lehenga?

The most inconvenient lesson has been this business of leading by example. It is such an underhand deal! Why can't I stay online while the children are offline? Why do I have to sleep well and eat healthy and sit up straight before my children do? Remember how our parents said, 'You can do what you like when you grow up'? Hello, this is cheating, I'd like to declare!

In all this, though, there has been a most unexpected gift—the wisdom of children. Kids remind us what we were like when we started out, what we can be like and what can be reclaimed. As Aliza once put it gently, 'I know everything already, but you have forgotten some things, Mamma.'

Children also have a natural sense of fairness and justice. All I need to do, as a parent, is trust them, so their trust in themselves is not damaged. This takes so much pressure off me.

'Everybody loves me,' said our youngest child. 'All the guests in our house love me.' She was four years old.

'That sounds like a good thing,' I replied. Something about her tone made me say this.

'I don't like that,' she complained.

'Why don't you like that?' I asked.

'Yesterday, after my aunt talked very nicely to me, she scolded her daughter a lot. I didn't like that.'

I held her close. Children look out for those who matter to them. They hurt when we hurt. They want to call out meanness and cruelty.

I must acknowledge my children's feelings when they express them. Be gentle, both as a listener and speaker, so they know they are valued.

Once more, I need to lead by example. Every now and then I pat myself on my back and say, 'Good job, woman. I'm impressed with you.'

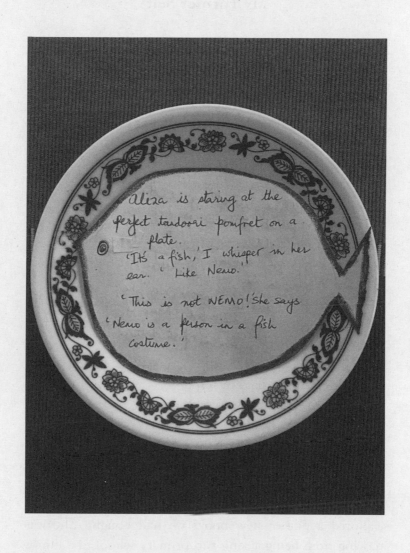

Sahar, the Firstborn, a Bridge to My Former Self

When I would dream of having children, Sahar is the daughter I would see by my side.

As our firstborn turned eleven, she walked into my room wearing a sleeveless shirt she had found on her own while searching for summer clothes. It was my shirt. I had outgrown it after Sahar was born.

Wearing that shirt, I had gone to work; chatted with my colleague in the basement office; been a professional news cameraperson; picked up equipment and filmed interviews. That shirt had made me feel triumphant.

There were no words, but I couldn't let go of Sahar as I held her in a tight hug.

'One thing I don't like about my mother is that when she is upset, she doesn't tell me why she is upset,' Sahar had written in a school essay when she was nine.

'We'll hold hands till our conversations come back,' I had written in my diary in response.

Our conversations are coming back. Stories that had gone silent in my head are returning. As our children grow up they help us recover from the exhaustion of being parents to very young offspring. They reassure us that we can get some rest now.

'Did you like middle school?' Sahar asked me as she explored a pile of new books we had bought. She was moving from being a senior in primary school to a junior in senior school.

I recalled the chaos of our class that had almost fifty students. The beauty and energy of some of my teachers. The wonder of studying geography and chemistry. Mrs Neera Sharma, our geography teacher, was so keen to teach us the details of the physical world, she would pick up speed towards the end of each period. I became a traveller in her class. Mrs Meera Maini, our graceful chemistry teacher, showed me everything a woman could be.

We talked about my misadventures with Sanskrit. I was terrible at remembering things I didn't understand. My attention would waver. I told Sahar that Sanskrit made me desperate. I made elaborate plans to cheat in exams.

'You cheated in school?' my daughter asked, wide-eyed.

'Yes, it was such a waste,' I said. 'During the exam, I was so scared, so tense. What if I get caught? How will I cope? What will my mother think?'

'How will my mother feel? There's always that,' Sahar whispered. I was startled to hear this about me.

'You worry about my reactions when you are in school?' I asked. I imagined myself as a laidback, permissive parent. Yet, there was a pile of expectations I seemed to have heaped on this child. She was wearing my clothes, but she was only eleven.

She asks very little of us, our firstborn. She is keenly attuned to my fragilities, and those of her father's. I know we will be better off when she gains the confidence to be more demanding. When she worries less about the breakdown one of us might have, trying to keep the balance from tipping over.

I speak to Sahar a lot more now about how I feel. I tell her stories of times when I was petrified but acted calm; times when I was so happy I couldn't stop my tears. She listens with her equanimous expression. I flaunt audacious dance moves as I brush my teeth. She covers her eyes and says, 'Oh god, where do you learn these things from!'

She asks us at the dinner table if we can go to Port Blair this summer. She was born in the capital city of the Andaman and Nicobar Islands. We often recount tales of our travels all over the Andamans with our first baby. She was introduced to the sea at Havelock. We explored Little Andaman with our baby wrapped snug in my blue bandhini dupatta. She wailed inconsolably as we waited in the open by a dock for a boat. It was getting cold and windy and I didn't know how to keep her warm. I felt shame at my inexperience, imagining that everyone was judging me.

So many stories. The times we lost our way home; the motorcycle rides interrupted by sudden rain; stopping at roadside dhabas to find a corner to nurse my baby—people scandalized at the sight of newbie parents travelling with such a small child. I learnt to let people stare. I practised my vacant smile in response to comments, advice and even reproof from random strangers.

How eager I had been to get everything right. How fearful I was of my beginner's ignorance.

We will go back, her father promises her. Sahar is disappointed it won't be soon enough. She wants to see where the story of her life began. She misses a piece of her own puzzle. We seek to build bridges that connect us to our former selves.

Perhaps this is why we, as parents, get so emotional at the visible milestones of our children growing up. Suddenly we come face-to-face with the lost parts of ourselves.

And then, we realize that instead of lamenting the loss, we have the option of recovering what-was.

As my daughter grows into the me I once knew, I grow closer to her as well. I come together, my pieces less scattered, more whole.

Because Balance Is Not Static

Shweta and I had not met each other yet. We knew each other only through our social media profiles—until I received her message in my Facebook inbox:

> I am at my Mom's home now and two weeks away from the due date. Arav is upset because he is here with me and missing his school and friends. He keeps telling me, "Once the baby is out, you can hug me hard and you can pick me up and you can bend down to tie my laces and you can stop drinking Digene."
>
> His world is disturbed by a baby he didn't plan. Yesterday I took him to the park and I couldn't catch up with him. He got so angry he told me he would take a knife and cut me in two. Later he cried. It completely broke my heart.
>
> Why do we have more than one child? Why do we go ahead and disturb the balance that we took so long to find?

I doubt very many of us think this through in a question-and-answer format. I sure hope not. We have a lifetime in front of us to notice clues, collect evidence and create connections that might explain why we are here in the first place. Why do we choose the spouse we do? Why is love not enough to make things work? Why do some friends come back? How do we learn to trust ourselves again? *Why do we disturb the balance we took so long to find?*

Because balance is not static, I wrote back to Shweta. My fingers seemed to be typing automatically.

We cannot 'find' equipoise and hold on to it forever. Seasons will change, disasters will strike, spring will come again. Everything is moving, evolving, growing, decaying around us constantly.

When I was pregnant with our second child, and I took my first work break, I found myself scouring the Internet for 'pregnancy + depression' to understand why I felt so low. I was not satisfied with anything that I read. My distress baffled me. I felt physically deflated. I couldn't bring myself to eat with the enthusiasm I had displayed during my first pregnancy. I felt lost. I searched for a simple answer that would knock me out of this depression. Nothing did.

By the time we reached the last trimester, our second baby had become a real child for me. She kicked and played inside me and reminded me to eat. I started wearing red for the first time in my life. I was large and red and waddling. And pleased with myself. The big, round, glowing face helped.

Aliza was born. The world started reminding us again how obsessed everyone was with gender. Without a second thought, I ignored the barbed comments and disappointment of others. In the delivery room, nurses had refused to respond to me when I asked whether the baby was a girl or a boy. I didn't need their answer. I recognized Aliza as soon as she was born. She cried in an odd, heavy voice. She was red-faced like a tomato. She was new, she was different, she had chosen us.

Three days later, my husband and I were sitting in a paediatrician's waiting room with our two daughters. I was holding our as-yet-unnamed infant in my arms.

Our firstborn and I seemed to have a private cocoon around us. We were one. We could be anywhere, in any setting, yet we were a self-contained island. Our personal universe was cozy and perfect.

Suddenly two-year-old Sahar walked off towards the play area in the clinic. She climbed on to a slide. And it happened. She walked out of our bubble. We were two separate people. We were no longer perfect. We weren't supposed to be perfect. We were free. We stretched ourselves in different directions, in a new light. It was a moment of liberation.

'She will heal us,' my husband had said when I first told him that I thought we might be pregnant a second time. 'She has liberated me,' I thought, the first time I stepped into the world with her.

And that was only the beginning.

The new baby will be the greatest gift your family will receive, I wrote to Shweta. She will bring courage and freedom. I know what I am talking about here. I am a second child myself. My father is nodding in agreement as he reads this right now.

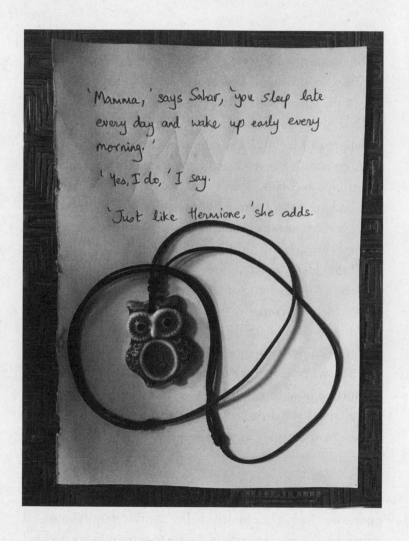

'Mamma,' says Sahar, 'you sleep late every day and wake up early every morning.'

'Yes, I do,' I say.

'Just like Hermione,' she adds.

Aliza, the Second, the Valiant Princess

'I know the meaning of Sahar, Aliza and Naseem, but what is the meaning of Natasha?' Aliza asked me.

We were sitting on high stools around a table in a café—before us, leftovers of pasta, pizza and pastries.

'Natasha means one who is loved by all,' I said. I make up whatever I feel like when I have to answer this question.

Aliza got off her stool and came to me. She put her arms around me and said, 'That's why all of us love you so much.'

I had an instant out-of-body experience. *This is real, this is real*, a voice reassured me. Aliza and our early interactions flashed through my mind.

There is so much about our children that we find ourselves unprepared for. I don't mean colic and diaper rash. I mean personality traits. World-view-things.

Aliza arrived with some gifts and talents that were actually unfamiliar to me. I could see them but it was not easy for me to recognize them. She seemed to have a clear version of how things had to be and she would demand compliance—she'd protest, negotiate, dig her heels in.

She would also celebrate the world as if it had just been invented.

Our second-born child was eager to start school. Yet, as she moved from playschool to nursery, our world cracked open—we had a newborn baby in the family—a third daughter. A week into starting to go to school, Aliza decided she wanted to stay at home.

Every nursery class has inbuilt chaos. Some children arrive crying. Some want to go home before the day ends. Everyone and everything is new. The anonymity is scary. 'I am okay in school,' Aliza told us, 'but I don't like to see other children cry.'

I reasoned with her, trying to offer an explanation that she might accept. I consoled her. Aliza was unconvinced.

In retrospect I see that Aliza's relationship with school and her sensitivity to the harshness of it was linked to Aliza's life at home.

A four-year-old caught between two siblings, Aliza was already feeling lost in the crowd. The atmosphere of school exaggerated that. She was desperately missing the love and protection of her parents, and school made her feel doubly vulnerable.

Aliza fought back. She became a princess. She insisted on wearing glittering dresses with golden borders and diamonds on her sandals. *Where is my magic wand? I demand my wings.* She refused the life we offered her.

Aliza and I became estranged and confused. We loved each other passionately, yet we could not reach out to one another. She threw tantrums. I started throwing tantrums in response. I hit her to make her stop screaming. I said horrible things. It would leave me in shock for days.

It must have been worse for her.

Sahar cowered in fear. The baby watched. Sometimes she would respond with anger and tears, too.

Why is Aliza so fragile? I would wonder. The answer came to me as another question. *Why are you so fragile, Natasha?*

Our recovery started when I calmed down and accepted Aliza's ways. We shut out every other voice to listen to her. A few days into staying at home with me, Aliza started self-schooling. She accepted the rules we made together—no watching cartoon films during school hours. She started painting, drawing and colouring. I labelled her works of art and put dates on them, hanging them on a string across our room.

At some point, Aliza started wearing cotton frocks and forgot all about the billowy satins with laces, the nets with red and gold roses that she had received as gifts. She was okay with being herself. We were both happy. Happier.

Some years later, the same Aliza—who had felt neglected, and who needed time off—hugged her mother in a café and made her feel like a princess.

Parenting. You've got to learn when to run and when to walk. Ears are useful.

The Happiness Key

'Sorry, Mamma, sorry,' Aliza came running to me one day, holding her ears. 'I'm sorry for all the wrongs I have done so far.' In one clean sweep, our four-year-old cancelled out a year full of tantrums after the birth of her little sister.

We've been growing up with our kids.

I call child-rearing a game because it inspires us to play. Play demands creativity, one gets better with practice and if one maintains the right spirit, there's laughter and fun. Play can also get difficult, it requires fitness and training.

We used to stay up nights sometimes, well into our twenties, playing Carrom or Bluffmaster—a group of cousins and friends. Partners would devise elaborate codes to communicate, scrutinize adversaries, look for clues in their every expression and make a move.

The same formula works with raising kids. Sahar has mostly spoken to us in words, except when she is drawing black flowers and playing with imaginary mice. Naseem comes with an agenda—'Never mind,' she seems to tell her sisters, 'you may have had a head start but I'll catch up soon.' Aliza has little patience; she will lie down on the floor and flap her arms. One day, she invented a happiness key. She jumped behind me and wound an imaginary key on my back. 'There, I have wound you, now be happy,' she commanded—enough of whatever I was moping over!

Yes, I had been miserable. I had lovely kids and a television job I loved. The kids and job loved me back. Yet, it didn't feel so good. I suffered from separation anxiety and felt like a fool for it. Confusion descended like a fog. I had no idea where the controls were. I had never really felt so lonely. Clearly, I had spread myself too thin; the urban myth of the supermom had trapped me. I looked good, but I felt terrible.

All at once, parenting proved to be a test of loyalty. Was I willing to be loyal to myself? I didn't have much practice in this area. It had always been easier to be loyal to friends, trends and gadgets.

I had to come to terms with a few grand truths. For one, I would be able to raise our kids well only if I first raised myself well. The same rules applied to adults and kids—sleep on time, eat well, don't make it a habit to get stuck in peak-hour traffic.

I also had to learn to pamper the child in me—love her, appreciate her, make her happy. When the parents are calm, the kids are happy. And vice versa. If my child is not okay, I can be sure that I'm not okay. It's a terrible thing to hear or accept when one has to run through the day chasing deadlines and appearing at meetings on time.

Over time, I learnt to do what I was good at, instead of compelling myself to do *everything*. Well-balanced meals bore me, but I can take photos. So I did. We hung out at the dosa corner in the market—and the photos, I shot them myself, with my very own loving hands. Those were as much a magic box of moments and memories as home-cooked nutritious meals might have been.

'I love Nani's rajma, Kanta Mausi's roti and Mamma's Maggi,' said Sahar. I learnt to receive compliments. When I was ready to pause, I noticed I was surrounded by love, adulation and gratitude. It was real.

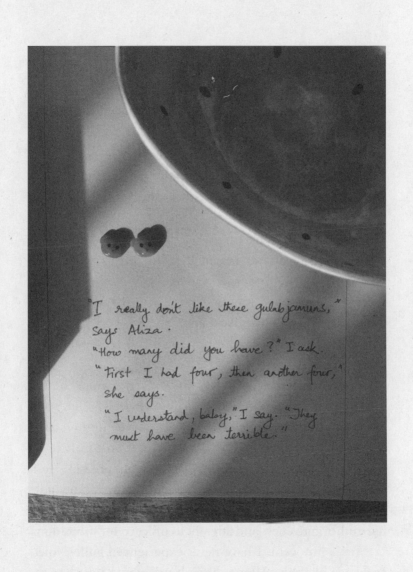

Naseem, the Youngest, All Magical Real

'Take a photo of me eating butter,' she said to me.

I obediently took a photo. The wide angle of the iPhone made the plate look larger than Ms six-year-old.

Naseem likes to lick us on our cheeks and arms in fits of affection. The rest of the family is disgusted by this act. I don't mind it very much. Actually, I love it! Although I must pretend to discourage her. Sometimes when I am holding her in the darkness, she quietly licks my hand once. It is a secret touch.

Naseem has a faux fur jacket shaped like a cape. It is a gift from my sister-in-law in Karachi. It has a 'Made in China' label. The first time Naseem wore it, she was three years old. She looked at herself in the mirror and exclaimed, 'Wow. I'm looking just like a dog!' She was very pleased. A friend of ours made an illustration of this happy moment of transformation.

Naseem says the darndest things. She wraps herself around our bodies. Sometimes she calls her father when he has been away for far too long and gives him a sound yelling. 'Come back quickly. You will not go to office on the day you are back. And I will hide your phone!' He is compelled to return a day early. True to her word, she hides his phone for a few hours so he cannot hear it ring. I look at her authoritativeness and attempt to unlearn my inhibitions.

She is innocent. I have never experienced guilelessness and trust like this. After a difficult pregnancy together, the miracle of her birth was the pinnacle of achievement for me. Time slowed down around us. We had no expectations except to just be. We were healthy. We were alive.

Naseem likes raw tomatoes. She often eats cucumbers as the main course of her meal. She loves grapes and berries. She collects dry leaves and stones and brings them to us as presents. We admire their textures, colours and shapes, their magical reality.

On a weekend morning walk, when we have nowhere particular to reach, she tells me that she really wants to have a pet animal. 'I want a small dog and a cat,' she says, cupping her palms together to hold an imaginary baby animal. 'In the beginning, the puppy will be small and I will hold it in my arms. Then, it will grow up and run around beside me.'

I imagine the puppy with her. She is my puppy for now. It is our shared joke. She often wags her imaginary tail at me. I wag mine back.

I call her all kinds of names. Namnam, Nanoo, Nanakuttu, Nonex. With her I have become more me. I have done what I want to do with her body stuck to mine. We edit images together—Naseem perched on my lap, giving me feedback. She chooses filters. She watches me struggle with PowerPoint presentations as she puts together a jigsaw puzzle by my side.

Naseem hasn't wrapped her head around the physical or political idea of a nation yet. She knows that India is home. We are Indians. She doesn't get how big or far-out India is. Every time she hears the name of a new place, she asks us, 'Is Bombay in India? Is Adilabad in India? Is Lucknow in India?'

'Yes,' we say.

'Oh,' she replies, trying to make a map in her head. She doesn't get artificial boundaries yet.

A while ago, it was vote-counting day after the general elections in this country. It was all very dramatic; the results came in early, and it was clear that Narendra Modi and the Bharatiya Janata Party had been voted in to form a new government at the centre.

When the children came home from school, we sat together at the dining table, eating fruits.

'*Ab ki baar*, Naseem *ki sarkar*,' I said as I passed a bowl of cherries to her.

'Who won, Mamma?' asked Aliza.

'Modi,' I said. 'Narendra Modi. The Congress party has been routed.'

'India,' asked Naseem, 'Mamma, did India win?'

Maths Oh Maths

For Aliza

$$7 + 9 + 7 + 9 = 32$$

$$7 + 8 + 8 + 9 = 32$$

$$8 \times 7 - 1/2 + 5 = 55$$

Aliza has shampoo-ed and conditioned her little sister's hair and is trying to cut a deal with her.

"When you grow up, you will have to get pachchas ice-creams for me," she says.

"What is pachchas?" asks Naseem.

"Fifty!"

"I only know counting till bees," says Naseem. "Twenty."

When Baby Aliza Spoke to Big Aliza

I am going to write this story in whispers. You know how it feels when something good happens after a very long time? I don't want to disturb the delicate, precious balance that exists—not even by exhaling out loud.

One of our children had become very quiet a few years ago. Then, she started talking again.

Aliza had a pre-birthday glow on her face. She had been studying calendars and counting down the days. We should buy a packet of toffees for my classmates, she reminded me.

When Aliza was still a baby, I used to call her Bob Christo. She was plump and bald and would go red and angry in the face when hungry. Besotted, I filmed videos of her and her older sister all the time.

'You have no time for Sahar and me ever since Aliza has come,' my husband would say. 'You don't love us any more!'

I would laugh and deny it. I would feel pride, without quite knowing what I was so proud about.

As a toddler, Aliza was a people magnet. She loved her food. She went on long walks with Rajni Didi, eating bananas and cheese slices all the way. She would return from school, change into her purple and gold sari, and ride her bicycle round and round the living room for hours.

Then, all at once, Aliza, our middle child, became very quiet.

It first started in school. She wouldn't talk to her teachers. She didn't like going on stage. She refused to perform, even in a group dance. 'I love to draw,' she said to me, 'but I don't want to take part in art competitions. Tell my teacher not to send me.'

At every parent-teacher meeting for almost three years, we heard the same feedback. 'She does all her work very well. She just never speaks. We can never get her to answer in class. That's all.'

On slow, quiet weekends, the home felt unusually silent, as though it were encased in fog. The sound of Aliza playing a tune on her Casio would connect us all. She wouldn't speak.

Often, it was just exasperating. 'Why don't you just say what you want? Why didn't you remind me when we were in the market? What's the point of this sorry face now?' I would lash out, inadvertently pushing her into a deeper cave of quiet.

Take yourself out of here, my inner voice would guide me. Go to the other room, lock yourself up, make a phone call . . . just stop being so distraught. She is not going to respond as long as you remain angry.

Friends of our family who had been fans of this child wondered at the change in her. Many guests would come and go without noticing her or interacting with her at all. It was easy to forget that she was there.

'Aliza will talk,' I would say, protectively. 'Just let her be. She has very strong opinions, she just doesn't have the words yet. She will find her voice again.'

As a toddler, Aliza had thrown the loudest tantrums. She was the one with the wisest repartees. She had also been the one I had yelled at the most.

Now, she had shut shop. Instinctively, I knew I shouldn't worry. I even identified with my girl. Her silence was a kind of resistance. In her quiet, she would find the means of recovering, too.

I spoke to her about how she had been as a toddler. 'One day we will make baby Aliza talk to big Aliza,' I said. She was mesmerized by the idea. We had an imaginary conversation with her younger self, hoping to help her connect with her inner vivaciousness. She looked like we had just plucked some magic out of the air around us.

Our lucky break came when Aliza discovered books. She would be hidden behind a Tintin comic for hours. She fell in love with Harry Potter. She would sit on the staircase with a J.K. Rowling book and laugh out loud at erratic intervals. She came to me with questions. 'What does this mean—"you have the emotional range of a teaspoon"?' My answer pleased her. Hermione became her new heroine.

Aliza began to recover in a physical way. She recovered best with her father. She'd climb over him as though he were a tree as soon as he returned home. Hug me properly, he'd say, trying to maintain his balance. This is my way, she'd answer, hoisting herself on to his shoulder. She'd used her fingers to turn his lips upwards into a smile, commanding him to laugh when she saw him frowning. She'd send him messages when he was away.

'Loving PAPA,' she typed to him on my phone one day, 'do you know who the vice president of India is? I know, I know, it is Mr Hamid Ansari and rafflesia is the largest flower in the world. Aliza.'

'When will we learn to read Urdu?' she asked him when he was back. She had begun to learn Kathak with her older sister. We saw her dance on her school stage for the first time. She stepped into the light and performed as if in a trance.

My fat, red baby is a graceful little woman now. A quiet child with a big goofy laugh.

Write It Now, She Said to Me

Sometimes, before one has acquired the clarity to ask the right question, the answer comes along.

'Why is your thumb in your mouth, Naseem?' I asked our two-year-old child. 'Are you afraid of Mamma?'

'Yes,' she nodded.

I saw it clearly, as if a fog had lifted. Naseem had first put her thumb in her mouth when she had been a few months old.

I opened a diary I maintained at the time and found an angry and despairing me in the words on the page. In that mental state, I was nursing Naseem. My mother would come and stay with us when my husband was travelling.

I look back and see Mum and me together on a bed, isolated. We could not talk. Mum wrapped in her own thoughts. Me, confused. The baby playing with a plastic doctor set. Naseem put her thumb in her mouth, sucking it for solace. I recognized her fear, her need for reassurance. Yet, I let her comfort herself.

We cannot solve all our problems all the time, every time. Some learning curves stretch gently over years.

Slowly, our toddler took many matters into her own hands. I was glad to let her. She and I were together and alone for hours every day. There are photos from back then that play as a slide show in my mind—Naseem sitting by the kerb outside our home, tracing squiggles on paper, with tomato seeds stuck to her cheek; baby and her puzzles strewn on the marble floor; a long, messy afternoon of watercolour art.

How can the best days of my life also be the worst days of my life, I'd wonder. I'd try making sense it, of Naseem and me, of her behaviour patterns. My moods.

Don't attack the symptoms, I remind myself these days. They are there for a reason. Let the malady reveal itself, only then will we heal. Some children eat for comfort. Some won't eat till they are comforted. Others fling themselves on the floor and throw tantrums. Many grown-ups do the same thing.

Letting Naseem suck her thumb in peace became a metaphor for healing.

I come from a family where we suppress our emotions. We suffer quietly and consider it a virtue to deny the hurt we may be feeling—wait, feeling? What feelings?

As someone who gets really, really worked up internally but doesn't let it show on the outside, I actually envy people who can externalize their stress—who show what they feel, when they feel it. It's a talent I need to recover.

I instinctively let Naseem lead the way. There was a kind of certainty in her manner, a natural rhythm of play and rest, a spontaneity that affected us all. When she put her thumb in her mouth to calm herself to sleep or let me know that she was hurt, I was glad she was able to help herself when no one else was available.

When Naseem was to turn five, I remember a moment in the car. All our children were in the back seat. We had left behind the city and the highway was taking us home.

Naseem was looking out at the setting sun from the car window. Her thumb was in her mouth.

'Namnoo Namnam,' I said to her, 'when you stop sucking your thumb for ever and ever, I will write about it.'

She pulled out her thumb from her mouth and wiped it on her frock. 'Write it now,' she said to me.

I'm an obedient mum, and I just did as I was told.

The Oldest Is Now the Youngest

The children called me when I was away from home on a work trip.

'Mamma, what time will you get back home on Thursday?' Aliza asked.

'11.30,' I said.

'11.30 in the morning?'

'No, 11.30 at night.'

'That means you will come on Friday,' she said.

'No, I will come on Thursday,' I replied.

'Okay, then get into bed with us,' she said. 'We will leave place for you. But by the time you get here, we'd have taken your place. I will write your name in your corner so you can get in anyway.'

'Why don't you write these essays for me?' I suggested. 'Sometimes you should do that, too.'

'I can't write your essays, Mamma. I have to write my Hindi debate.'

Then, our firstborn Sahar—who had turned eleven—came on the phone.

'Sahar, I want to write an essay on you,' I said.

'Then write it,' she smiled.

'Should I write about our fights also?'

'Yes,' she said. 'It's okay to fight.'

'It's okay,' I repeated.

'Yes, Mamma, it's much better after Papa and you fight. Otherwise there is too much tension, you know—when you're not saying anything but there's something on your mind.'

Our youngest child—back then, all of six—was next.

'Hakuna Matata,' Naseem said and giggled. I put the phone on speaker so her voice filled my hotel room.

'Hakuna Matateeee,' she repeated and ran off to play.

'You live in a jungle,' I told my husband when he managed to get the phone at the very end. He laughed.

I returned home with a new idea. I told my family that Sahar was now six and Naseem, eleven. The youngest would be treated like the oldest and the oldest like our baby.

On Sahar's second birthday, she was already the big sister of a two-month-old Aliza. She was still a toddler, but for me, she was a little lady—wise and stoic. I depended on her to support me.

I had always been proud of how connected Sahar and I were. After we became a family with three children, I seriously expected my firstborn to help me keep things together. She was five.

When our youngest child turned six, I began to look back at the time when Sahar was her age. I marvelled at how different their lives were. Naseem is a carefree child, demanding what she wants and knowing how to get it. Then, there's Sahar—controlled and responsible as the big sister of two younger siblings.

Suddenly, Sahar began to switch from angelic to crabby. She began to fall ill a lot. I wrote in my diary that Sahar is the key. When she is fine, we are fine. When she is moody and irritated, something is not okay with what we are doing together as a family.

I could see how much pressure we were piling on to her and how unfair it was. I wanted to stop.

'Sometimes when you are being angry with me, in my mind I call you bad names,' Sahar confessed to me one day. She was crying.

'What do you call me?' I asked.

'I call you a *sada hua karela*,' she said. A rotten bitter gourd.

I could understand her despair. I could feel it, too. She didn't know how to ask for anything that she wanted with the confidence that she deserved it. She assumed everyone would simply say no to her. We didn't realize it, but we did say no to her a lot.

I was reminded of a time when she was my toddler. I was newly married and a new mother. I felt threatened and vulnerable, yet I invested a lot in keeping up pretences. There would be a tight knot in my stomach, even as I would wear my everything-is-so-perfect mask. We had to look good, no matter what. We had to make do with what we had and present a cheerful, brave face.

Of course, my mask would crack when I was alone with Sahar. She has witnessed the worst of me. It's another secret bond between us.

Over the last few years, Sahar has learnt to throw tantrums in her own way. She leaves the scene of conflict quietly, then she stomps all the way up the stairs and lets us hear her grunts from her study.

I hold myself back from reacting in anger. Back off, Natasha, I say to myself. Everything isn't about you. Give her space to lose control, to be unreasonable. Let her know that it is safe to express anger.

We don't always recognize the sadness and confusion children feel as they try to make sense of the world they have little control over.

When Sahar throws a tantrum these days, I know that we are doing something right. It's time for her to be the baby in the family.

'Are you a rabbit or a porcupine?' I would ask Sahar sometimes when she was younger.

'I'm a porcupine right now,' she would hiss at me.

I would be reminded that if you forget to hug a rabbit for too long, you have to deal with a porcupine for a little while.

Tight Hugs Four Times a Day

I'm writing this to find a way of starting a conversation with my daughter—my middle daughter.

As her older sister grows into adolescence, I have been especially alert to her needs. Our youngest is bubbly and vivacious and does interesting things like bringing us flowers and pebbles from the garden or throwing herself on the floor in despair, exclaiming, 'Mamma, *main kyaaa karoon*— what should I do?' She gets our attention. Mostly positively, sometimes negatively.

Our middle child, Aliza, is quiet and thoughtful. She likes football and cycling. She loves to read. I rarely have the time to listen to stories from her books. She has a repertoire of jokes, but she almost always lets her sisters take over the narration and punchlines. She is deep and mysterious.

Aliza hates change. Her comfort is constancy. She craves chocolate and cheese. Her father responds to that need. She yearns for new books regularly. Her mother responds to that need. She reads the dictionary in her spare time, discovering words that make her wonder.

'Mamma, what is the word for the person who wants to know everything?' she asked me one day.

'Nerd,' I replied.

She smiled.

'Are you a nerd?'

'Yes,' she said. 'Can we go to the Science Museum?'

'No,' groaned her sister before I could react.

One day, I snapped at her. It was late in the evening. Just the kids and I were at home, and suddenly, I reached the end of my tether. In response, Aliza snapped back—worse than me, leaving me confused. What was going on here? She wouldn't let me make amends afterwards.

Aliza doesn't ask for much. This is not healthy. When she is hurt, she withdraws for a very long time. She becomes dull and inattentive; even absent-minded. She can't find anything. She doesn't clear out her school bag. She seems to be carrying a burden. In her sleep, she yells and throws about her arms and legs.

Aliza is very articulate, but when she must express emotions, it is through non-verbal cues.

She jumps on her father and hugs him, making him lose his balance. But she is independent and self-sufficient around me. She and I rarely hug or even touch each other.

After the flare-up, I woke up in the middle of the night wondering why my middle child seemed depressed. What had I done? Had I been sad around her? Had I been overburdened and harsh? (Yes and yes.) My daughter was keeping out of my way. I had been exactly like her when I was twelve. And it was terrible.

What a tattered, boring old script I was confronting: 'No one is ever going to approve of you at home, so look for temporary homes elsewhere.' I would be stupid to pass this message down to another generation.

Unable to reach out to my daughter, I got into her single bed with her and held her as she slept. By 3 am, she had spread out her legs and arms and thrown me out of her bed.

Just after our showdown, I had asked Aliza to call her father, and speak to him. She tried to explain her moods to him in chronological order: 'I was okay in the morning, then we went to see a film, I was okay after that also, but then I don't know what happened . . .'

She didn't tell him that I had yelled at her. 'Why do you act so dull, Aliza?' I had said, pushing her further into her shell.

I had been tired. Tired of being alone. Tired of holidays. My laptop had gone for repair, and I was tired of reading off my phone. Just temporarily exhausted. I exercised my right to yell.

It's a mindless assumption. No one has the privilege to raise their voice. Not the frustrated father and not the self-styled self-sacrificing mother. Go to your room and nap, or go out and talk on the phone. Please don't pile on to your children. They are not in control either.

The morning after, I went back to Aliza's room to wake her up. Her voice had recovered its gentle quality. She was fresh. She squinted, coming to terms with the April morning light. I walked out of the room, as though my work was done.

Then, I remembered that I hadn't done my real work. I went back.

'Aliza, are you better now?'

'Yes, Mamma.'

'Give me a hug.'

She did.

Aliza gives world-famous bear hugs. It is her special talent.

She was on the bed and she wrapped herself around my waist. I bent my neck to kiss her forehead. Her hair.

'From now on, you and I have to hug each other four times a day every day.'

She nodded.

'Okay?'

'Yes, Mamma.'

Two days later, we went to the Science Museum. It was liberating. I had no agenda, except to enjoy myself with my daughter. She ran from room to room, curious and full of fun. I had turned off the mobile data on my phone, so there was no need to bring it out of my bag except to see the time.

The next morning is the start of a new term in her school. I give Aliza a tight hug and kiss as she gets out of the car wearing an oversized school bag full of new course books.

'That's the third hug for today,' she tells me. She is keeping count.

It's not very complicated, I realize, when you simplify it.

"My roti is a cokodyle,"
Naseem opens its jaw.

"Mine is a fan."
Sahar flutters it
near her face.

"I'm making a cupcake,"
Aliza bites her roti into
shape.

When We Slow Down and Do Nothing

I was at home with fever, whining and moaning in the same room as my children. I asked our youngest, Naseem, for help.

'Ohoo hoo hoo. I'm not well, Namnoo. Make me well,' I said.

She looked up from her puzzle. 'I cannot make you well, Mamma. Go and see a doctor.'

'You can make me feel better, jaanoo. Say something nice to me.'

She came to me. She caressed my hair. 'Lie down. You will feel better. Do you want a hug?'

I received a hug. I lay down. I felt better.

Another winter afternoon, our three children are playing in the parking lot outside our home. Laughter, energy, dust and sunshine. The youngest is speaking loudly; there's complete synergy between her and the middle child. Sahar, the eldest, is quiet. She seems to be somewhere else. She has outgrown her trousers and they now end too soon before her ankles. There are so many photos of her wearing pyjamas like that.

When our second child was born, Sahar had come to meet me in my hospital room, holding my mother's hand, like a little woman. When we returned home, she spent endless afternoons watching the video '*Yeh taara, woh taara, har taara*' from the film *Swades*, on loop. In the background, I'd be looking after our new baby.

In a home video we sometimes watch, two-year-old Sahar

wakes up from sleep, comes towards me for a hug, then stops and says, 'Mamma will feel hurt, no, if I come too close to her?' We all know this dialogue by heart, spoken in a toddler's sleep-coated, sing-song, plaintive voice.

At two, Sahar had been my perfect travel companion as we returned home to Delhi, cutting short a holiday in San Francisco. Her father had met with an accident and was recovering after a surgery in Delhi. Between take-off and landing, Sahar and I were to spend forty hours on flights and in airports. Balancing four-month-old Aliza on my chest in a baby carrier, and pushing a trolley laden with bags and a stroller, Sahar and I wandered around the airport in Singapore looking for transit hotel rooms. She walked next to me, studying my face, as I read signs and maps, trying to find our way in the middle of the night.

'Have we come the wrong way?' she would ask me every now and again. That two-year-old voice, concerned for us, trying to support and reassure me, is embedded in my memory. I had said to her before starting our journey, 'You and I, Sahar, we are a team.'

Our family's big challenge arrived when our third child was born. Sometimes we were just a bunch of scared, lost people in the same space. We were doing so much, yet it felt like we were getting nowhere. I was gentle and loving with the baby; my voice would always soften when I looked at her. Yet, I felt depleted and dissatisfied with everyone else. My children had not met this angry, edgy version of me before—and she seemed like she was here to stay.

Sometimes, it's a long time after one has crossed a

threshold that one realizes how far one has come—here's our baby now playing the big boss; the Papa turning into the Mamma; and the big girl getting to be the baby she missed out on being. Instinctively, I hold the older children more as the youngest jumps off my lap to conquer her world.

When did we change?

Maybe, when we slow down and do absolutely nothing, things happen by themselves.

'Naseem,' I call out to my daughter. 'Tell me what to write in this essay.'

'I don't know,' she says. 'I don't even know how to write.'

'Should we draw something?'

'Look, Mamma,' she is suddenly distracted. 'The light is shining in that corner. Get your camera. Quick. Take a photo.'

The leaves of the plant by the windowsill are aglow. A shaft of light is making its way through them.

Learning to Listen to Innocence

Zoraz was already wearing a few rakhis on his wrist when he arrived with his mother for a family get-together at our home. Seven-year-old Zoraz lives in the US and was on his annual holiday to India to meet his grandparents and an assorted collection of relatives.

It was Raksha Bandhan and there were still some new rakhis lying at home. Zoraz wanted the rakhis—*all* of them—on his wrist. In the whirl of dinner and after-dinner cake and Tambola games, we forgot about his request.

At 11 pm, Zoraz approached me, and spoke in Hindi. 'You said my sisters would tie me a rakhi,' he whispered.

'We can do it tomorrow,' I shrugged.

'But it will finish today,' he explained, framing his sentence slowly. 'It won't be Raksha Bandhan tomorrow.'

I understood his request and got our daughters together. All of them tied the rakhis on Zoraz's wrist. He went to his mother Sana and insisted that he had to give money to each of them. I tried to intervene. Sana looked at me and asked how we could argue with her son when he had such clear notions about how the festival must be celebrated.

The next morning, even while surrounded by extended family members, I talked to my twelve-year-old daughter and mentioned the forthcoming festival of Bakr Eid.

'Oh, that's so sad,' said Zoraz, looking up from the game he was playing.

'What is sad, Zoraz?' I asked.

'I feel sad on Bakr Eid. I don't like sacrificing the goat. It is terrible.'

'I feel sad, too,' I admitted. 'But I am not allowed to say it. I have to pretend to be happy.'

Zoraz looked at me in wonder. 'Why can't you say it?'

'You know, the best thing about being a child is that you can say what you feel.'

'You can't say what you feel?' he asked me. Zoraz has light-green doe-like eyes.

'Sometimes grown-ups have to keep their feelings to themselves because people can get offended by them,' I said to him. 'But you don't worry about that.'

Something about Zoraz's expression—its absolute purity— and his desire to establish a connection with a family he rarely met overwhelmed me. We should trust ourselves much more than we do, I made a note to myself.

'Mamma,' said Sahar, a few weeks later, 'do you know that in that film—*Inside Out*—our emotions are shown as real people inside our heads? All the emotions in the father's brain are male, the ones in the mother's brain are female, but the ones in the child's brain are both male and female.'

'Yes,' I acknowledged. 'As we grow up there is far too much pressure to be only one kind of person. We taunt and shame each other until we fit into boxes—become limited people.'

Twelve-year-old Sahar was worried that some of her friends were growing too fast into teenagers. She had read a fair number of comics—*Archie* and *Barbie*—to know what teenagers were supposed to be like. She was resisting peer pressure—the expectation that she had to behave in a manner that was considered age-, class- and gender-appropriate.

In solidarity, I put a photo of her as a seven-year-old child on the desktop of our home computer.

Listen to the children, I remind myself. It is the least we owe to the people who are always listening to us.

Wait. What did I just say there? Children *don't* listen to us! This is the complaint every parent seems to have. Yet, when I look at our kids looking at us, I feel like I can hear the laser scanner in their brain going *wzzz-wzzz* as it copies everything it sees and hears.

It is not easy to listen to children. Our patriarchal family setup has taught us that they are not supposed to matter. We are meant to train and mould them into proper human beings. We expect resistance, as if they are a lower form of life. Their innocence and clear-eyed insights are misconstrued for a lack of intelligence.

Ever since the demise of their grandmother, the topic of death had been coming up quite frequently in my children's conversations at home. Sahar told us about a story she had in mind for a film she wants to make when she grows up.

'After people die, they will go to heaven, where there will be no class or caste divisions. All those we ignored when we were on earth will be our equals and we will discover how interesting they are. There will be complete equality.

'People will live like this for 150 years before they are reborn,' she concluded.

Naseem, almost seven, did some quick mathematical calculations in her head. 'When you die, Mamma, you will be in heaven for 150 years. When I die and come there, you will have been reborn. You won't be there any more. I will take a video game from an angel and put you into it as a character. Then I will play you and steer you and take you to the treasure you are looking for.

'And you will say, "*Arre wah*, how did I find this treasure!"'

My daughter looked like she had already found her precious hoard—as she imagined herself running my life from a heaven above.

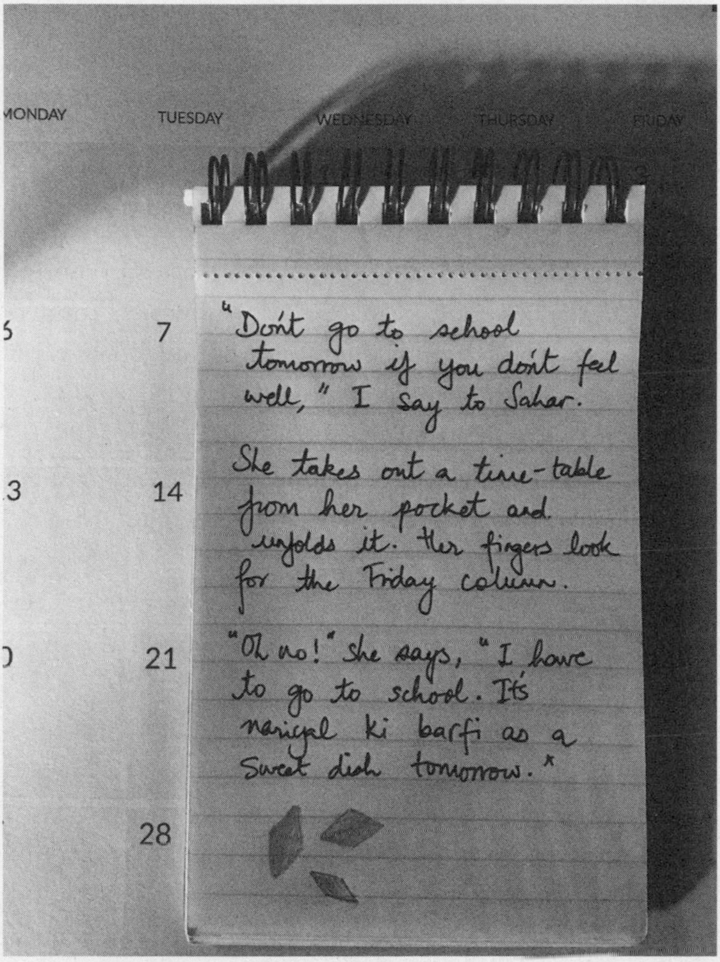
MONDAY
TUESDAY
WEDNESDAY
THURSDAY
7
14
21
28
"Don't go to school tomorrow if you don't feel well," I say to Sahar.
She takes out a time-table from her pocket and unfolds it. Her fingers look for the Friday column.
"Oh no!" she says, "I have to go to school. It's nariyal ki barfi as a sweet dish tomorrow."

A Technology Chowkidar at Home

'Mamma, you are checking your phone like I put my thumb in my mouth,' said my six-year-old daughter, Naseem. Both of us were on the floor, trying to reassemble a 200-piece jigsaw puzzle.

She was right. Bang on. My smartphone was my pacifier.

Perhaps I felt vulnerable. Perhaps I was overcommitted. I have not aced time management. So, instead of being present in the moment, I longed to be online and connect with people who weren't there, so I could temporarily disconnect from the people who *were* physically around.

I browse the Facebook and Twitter apps on my smartphone a lot less when I am alone. I reach for them more frequently when there are lots of people at home. Sometimes it really is like the stiff drink I might have hidden behind the house plants. I take a quick sip to keep the buzz in my head, and help me stay aloof from the chaos around me.

My husband often calls himself a Luddite. Afzal uses his iPhone only to make phone calls. Besides the car and his phone, the gadget he uses the most on any given day is usually the electric mosquito swatter. Have you ever used one? The crackly sound of a mosquito being stalled mid-flight is addictive. Even mosquitoes are drawn to it, I think.

We got rid of the television in our home in the early years of our marriage. Between work, home, babies and guests, I had no time for it. My work involved creating and watching television all the time. I didn't need more of the same thing at home. If it happened to be switched on elsewhere, Afzal would stare at the TV screen like a deer trapped in headlights. Out of sight, out of mind—this worked for us when we were home together.

Despite my own intense love for gadgets—computers, cameras, smartphones and the mini electric food chopper—I am the tech chowkidar in our home, the self-appointed watchman who moderates access to technology in family spaces. In the process of making checks, I often summarily delay the entry of bona fide candidates. My own first iPhone lay in its case for over a year before I got a sim card for it. Our children were still babies, and I knew that I had to delay this inevitable love affair. Often, I feel compelled to acquire the latest gadget and keep it only for myself—purely for professional reasons, of course.

As a parent, it is critical for me to keep superfluous technology out of our lives. There are so many of us already in our home—three busy children and two grown-up children masquerading as their parents. We barely listen to each other. We are often way behind in keeping track of each other's creative milestones. Someone has learnt a new poem, another has made a drawing, a third has had a dramatic encounter with something in the garden, and we all need some time to share our experiences with each other.

So we do things that may seem odd to other families. Ours is an iPad-free residence. We have no video game consoles. Until a while ago, we did not have Wi-Fi either. I deliberately used a slow and fragile dongle to dial-up when

I needed to. We have a television screen on the wall, but we don't have a cable connection. We miss all the latest films and popular series. We watch movies of our choice on DVDs and via pen drives. No advertisements play in our home. None of us has seen an Indian Premier League match. We go to doctors' waiting rooms and ask for the TV remote first. We switch from the usual news channels to wildlife programming, which is also increasingly becoming violent in its content.

It's not so much technology as it is the onslaught of manipulative and mindless content that we reject. None of us can recognize Taylor Swift, Rohit Sharma or Sunny Leone. (I had to google a few keywords to recall Rohit and Sunny's names for this sentence.) No one in my family can tell you what 'GoT' stands for. We miss trends, but they die out so soon that you wouldn't really find out that we didn't know what you assumed we must have known when it was the thing to know.

Sure, we seem as smart and well-informed as our peers. It has not been very difficult to pull this off.

Let me throw in some jargon. I do not want us to be a family of Western-consumerist-culture-addicted-Anglophones. We don't want to find ourselves scavenging for comfort amid the clutter of shallow, raucous media content with limited shelf life.

I want variety in our lives. Slowness. Pauses. Daydreaming and imaginary friends. I don't want to prepare our children for the 'real world'. I want us and them to have the confidence that we can create the world we want to live in.

We don't have to fit into pre-fabricated moulds. We are free to discover and relate to our inner and outer worlds at our own pace. We can pick and choose. This is real life.

A while ago, we had attended a live music concert in New Delhi at which Harpreet, a young musician, sang soulful Punjabi folk and semi-classical songs to mark the release of his first album *Ajab Ishq Maati Da*. Our children had not been entirely convinced that they wanted to attend this. Their grandparents' home, where they could play video games and watch TV, had seemed a more attractive and relaxing alternative.

There was no iPad in the car as we negotiated rush-hour traffic to reach the venue. The children did not have smartphones to fiddle with as we took our seats and waited for the programme to start. They sat among strangers and adults and waited for the lights to dim and the music to start. We stayed connected and attentive to each other.

After the concert, Aliza repeatedly chose to play the same songs by Harpreet in the car and at home. It was not 'cool' to be hooked to such music at their age, but the experience of hearing it live had touched them. The children engaged with the lyrics, the vocals and the guitar riffs. Could I have planned this deep connect between them and song? Did I know the outcome when I was being the ruthless chowkidar, controlling everyone's choices? I didn't, but I still take the risk of boring them regularly with the confidence that lying fallow will lead to being fertile.

Learning takes time. Don't give up your entitlement to your own time.

Less is more. We have to resist the nagging feeling that we are missing out if we don't constantly try to keep up with the trends of the day. We can choose to engage deeply with what speaks to us rather than skim over things because there is too much to catch up with.

When we create a deliberate absence of easy distractions in our children's lives, it means that we have to fill these spaces with our own presence. My children and I—we entertain each other. We create and perform the content that would otherwise be available via gadgets.

This means that I have to be my own watchman. I switch off notifications and put away my smartphone.

This was my plan all along.

Small Doses of Joy

Sometimes misery is a just a faded old security blanket. It has been useful for so long that you don't have the heart to get rid of it. Besides, who knows, you might need it again.

When I was asked to write of happiness recently, I realized I was in big trouble. If I confronted and accepted my happiness in print, there'd be no going back—I'd be doomed to remain happy forever.

How would I like that?

No, man. No way. I like my happiness in small doses.

The truth is I am a needy, miserable fool. Just like most of us. Only I am worse. I work from home. No work gets done at home. I miss my friends. I miss deadlines. I want to be at the airport. I want frothy coffee by a window. I hate net-banking. I hate real banking even more. The doorbell rings. I am depressed, I think. Or shallow. Or both.

There is jalebi in the kitchen. There is a little girl in the house. Naseem. She is by my knee now.

'Mamma, listen,' she says, her podgy little hand on her heart.

I put my left hand on her heart, my right hand still on my mouse.

'Dhak-dhak, dhak-dhak,' says Naseem.

'What?' I ask, almost whispering.

'God likes jalebi,' she whispers back. 'I just had jalebi and my heart is beating loudly. Listen.'

What do I do with this moment? Somewhere in here is the meaning of life being handed to me on a platter.

As a college student, I used to be one of those irritatingly cheerful people. 'Turn off your face, Natasha,' my friends would say. 'It's too early in the morning.'

But I really came into my element in the most miserable phase of my life. I quit my beloved job. The children went to school. The husband went out of town. My Internet connection collapsed. Who am I? Where am I? Where are my people, I cried.

Fade to black.

I must remind myself of essential life lessons.

For one, there is no 'formula' for happiness—not love, not success, not children and not even pasta. Picking guavas off the tree comes pretty close.

Taking decisions is easy. It's the C-word that spells trouble—'commitment'. Committing to a decision. Commitment is hard work. It can make grown-ups cry.

I must also admit to something peculiar. I can appear sad on the outside, but I can be perfectly happy inside. I know I am in the right place, at the right time, with the right people. Little beautiful moments flash before me every day till I celebrate them. In other words, just because I am miserable doesn't mean I can't be happy. Contrary feelings co-exist.

If there is sorrow, it must persist for a reason. Let me not mess with it too much. There's a wiser, quieter, happier me lurking within. I must let her lead the way.

Happiness is a decision. It is an innate need, a survival strategy. I must be happy despite the onslaught of reality. I must hold on to joy in defiance of the ugly world that surrounds us.

Wait, there is an interruption. Little Naseem is here with her doctor set.

'I want to do your makeup,' she says.

'Check-up?' I ask.

'Yes, check-up,' she says. She uses her stethoscope on me, its pink heart makes a beep.

'Show me your elbow,' she says.

'You mean knee,' I whisper.

'Yes,' she answers, 'I want to pack-up your knee.'

'Check-up,' I say.

She knocks a plastic hammer on my knee.

I am well, it seems.

Miracles stalk us, they creep up on us—through a song, a smile, the play of light.

Let the small moments embrace you. And make you joyous.

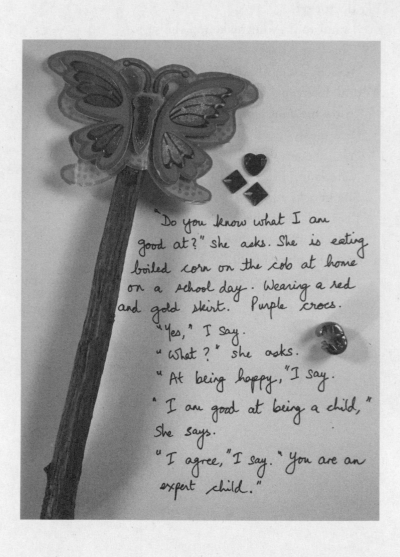

"Do you know what I am good at?" she asks. She is eating boiled corn on the cob at home on a school day. Wearing a red and gold skirt. Purple crocs.

"Yes," I say.

"What?" she asks.

"At being happy," I say.

"I am good at being a child," she says.

"I agree," I say. "You are an expert child."

Receiving Is a Form of Generosity

As a schoolgirl, when I had first read Kahlil Gibran, I wanted to make posters of his words and paste them everywhere. My parents' bedroom door was one of the designated spots, particularly for this:

> *Your children are not your children.*
> *They are the sons and daughters of Life's longing for itself.*
> *They come through you but not from you [. . .]*

Soon, our firstborn will be appearing for her final examinations in school. Exams make me restless. If I stay calm and uninvolved, I feel guilty—as though I'm being callous. I become more comfortable when I get into a tizzy with stress and performance anxiety, even though it is the child who has to appear for the exams.

By the time I turned twelve, school exams had become a recurring nightmare—a matter of life and death. I had interpreted my parents' anxious comments about our performance in school quite literally. Often, I'd tell my friends that if I fared poorly, my folks would kill me.

We all spoke like that. One of my closest friends would quote her father—that he was willing to sell his bones to ensure that his children got a good education. The intense but ridiculous image conjured by those words has stayed with me.

A large part of my journey as a parent has entailed unlearning all that I have absorbed from the family I grew up in, and granting myself the freedom to learn from the little people who are my new family. It is my turn to attend to the words of Kahlil Gibran:

> *You may house their bodies but not their souls,*
> *For their souls dwell in the house of tomorrow,*
> *which you cannot visit, not even in your dreams.*
> *You may strive to be like them,*
> *but seek not to make them like you [. . .]*

Here are five unexpected lessons I learnt when I looked to my children for answers.

Trust children

Trust kids to know what they want to do, and how they wish to do it. This has taught me to trust myself.

There is way too much loose talk in our culture about children being selfish and manipulative. We label them even before we have had a chance to know them. Trusting our children and ourselves is a position that goes against the spirit of the extended family. It goes against the grain of the school system.

It suits everyone when we are hesitant and doubtful, rather than intuitive. We are expected to toe the conventional line out of fear.

Don't let yourself be overawed. The answers are within you. They lie within your children. Trust is powerful.

Let your children protect you

Children yearn to care for and support us, and express this with startling intensity. They map our emotions all the time and try to see how they can make it easier for us. This is what family means, and children know it better than adults.

The emotional expression of children is less timid and contaminated than that of grown-ups. Don't make the mistake of rejecting their love.

Accept kids' gratitude

Some of us are so scared we are unlovable that we are unable to receive love even from our own children.

Children are persistent. They plant kisses and give us compliments. They're guileless—and when we open ourselves to them, their innocence can touch us unexpectedly. Still, some of us are foolish enough to mistrust their gestures.

Be a child with your children instead of always expecting them to be grown-ups in your company.

Ask children for help

This is a really big one for me. After years of being overwhelmed and judging myself for my inadequacies, I have learnt to ask my children for help all the time.

I bring them back from school after an intense workday and tell them that I need a nap. I ask them to help each other. I swat away the guilt that buzzes around me like an annoying mosquito and teach myself to rest. Being exhausted is *so* last century.

Giving without accepting anything in return embitters relationships. It tires us as parents. Receiving is also a form of generosity.

Love yourself like you love your child

It will all begin to balance out.

Take care of yourself with responsibility and you won't resent having to care for young children. If you want your child to appear for examinations with confidence, teach yourself to de-stress first.

So, here I am, keeping myself thoroughly distracted, while my daughter watches her favourite films during study leave.

> *You are the bows from which your children*
> *as living arrows are sent forth [. . .]*
> *Let your bending in the archer's hand be for gladness;*
> *For even as He loves the arrow that flies,*
> *so He loves also the bow that is stable.*

My Parents' Daughter

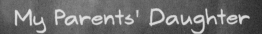

"Mamma, which year were you born in?"

"Nineteen seven ---"

"NINETEEN! NINETEEN? Oh God, Mamma, oh God!"

Coming Home to Become My Mother

Guddi. When my mother tries to excitedly explain something to me, she calls me Guddi.

Guddi is not my name. Guddi Massi is my mother's younger sister—the one she grew up with and later wrote letters to on inland cards that cost 35 paise. Guddi is everyone's favourite aunt.

I used to correct Mum and say, 'I am not Guddi!' Now I realize what an honour it is to be called that—my mother's sister. My mother's favourite person.

It was Mother's Day. My daughters surprised me with cards. I opened them to find little pink hearts and other cheerful illustrations of their love. It made me stop everything and sit down. The cards reminded me that underneath the confidence I display, is a tight knot of fear—fear that my children will resent me, that they will judge us. Harshly.

I've never said very nice things to my own mother. It isn't easy. Yet, how hard can it be, really? What am I waiting for?

'It is not important to know why. It is more important to stop,' my teacher would say, to steer us away from empty analysis and towards positive action.

My mother laughs very loudly. When she gets together with her siblings and friends, we can hear her voice from a safe distance. As a teenager, it used to embarrass me. Then, I grew up and learnt how to laugh with abandon, too. Sometimes my middle child gives me the look, hinting that I tone down my excitement.

My mother and my husband get along like old friends— it's as though they've always known each other. They talk about investments and business strategy. She tells him stories of her father's incredible adventures and her mother's multiple talents. As I overhear them, comparing notes on the cows and buffaloes and summer fruits of their childhood homes, I feel mildly jealous.

I had thought we had little in common—my husband and I—and then, I look at my parent and spouse, chatting like long-lost friends. She asks him about his plans, he tells her stories, then she informs him that her father had done similar things. I haven't met her father, my grandfather. Apparently, I have fallen in love with a man quite like him. I wonder at the wonder of it.

My mother is also the mother of my two brothers. When Bhai and I get together, we still fight over Mum. We tattle to her when the other is not around. Confused, Mum tells him what I say, and informs me about his comments. 'Sort it out, you two, and get out of my hair now,' she seems to be urging us, showering attention instead on her grandchildren.

They are good sons, my mother's children. My brothers. They've been brought up well.

My mother is a best friend. She extends herself effortlessly. She is an enabling presence.

The first time I saw my mother when I looked into a mirror, it startled me. I was getting ready for my wedding. My friend Reena had tied up my hair and done my makeup. Oh my god, it was my mother looking back at me—my mother from her wedding album. How was it even possible? We weren't supposed to be alike.

The first time I really began to feel like Mum was when our third child was born. All my life I had travelled and worked and achieved like my father and now I was coming home to become my mother. I borrowed the ring she had always worn and slipped it around my finger. I looked at my hands doing things like Mum. I began to learn how to be the woman I had always avoided becoming. Let the hurt of the past run through a sieve. What you're left with is the power you have inherited.

I became my mother's daughter. The one who gets things done. Gently. Firmly.

I have learnt a lot about patience and generosity from my mother. On my part, I show her how to be assertive, to express what she knows is true.

It isn't such a big deal, I've learnt. There's a graceful mother hidden behind the awkward, under-confident one. You know she has that beautiful, ringing laugh in her. Discover it within yourself, too. It will startle so much else into wakefulness.

To Fail without Feeling Like a Failure

When I was a kid, I used to lie, cheat and steal.

It is a useful memory to hold on to as a parent. There's not very much my daughters can do that I have not already done, I reassure myself. Their adventure-hunting father has covered the remaining range of possibilities.

There came a time when I began to find things in my daughter's pockets—crayons from school or some money. I chanced upon a packet of biscuits in the drawer of her study desk.

I stayed calm. It's all right, all kids steal. I recounted to my husband that I once got home a whole classmate, just to check the outer limits of my power as a six-year-old. 'It is normal for a very young child to take something which excites his or her interest,' Google confirmed in 0.27 seconds.

Yet, there was the unmistakable soundtrack of panic galloping towards me. Despite my highfalutin decisions to rewrite the family script, I had to be doing something exactly like my parents, for my child to be behaving like I had at her age. I walked into the park next door to breathe out a silent scream.

A while ago, I read an excerpt from Amy Chua's *Battle Hymn of the Tiger Mother*, where she explained how Chinese parents produced successful kids. Her bluntness and clarity was a hook, but I was also amused by the self-parody and wry humour. I shared the article online. That is when I began to realize the enormity of what this piece was doing to its readers. It was dredging up anger, fear, self-doubt, judgement and passionate counter-arguments.

Describing how she pushed her seven-year-old Lulu to master a piano piece, Amy Chua wrote:

> I threatened her with no lunch, no dinner, no Christmas or Hanukkah presents, no birthday parties for two, three, four years. When she still kept playing it wrong, I told her she was purposely working herself into a frenzy because she was secretly afraid she couldn't do it. I told her to stop being lazy, cowardly, self-indulgent and pathetic [. . .]

Amy Chua clarified in interviews that her book was the story of her own eventual transformation as a mother. 'Mine is a cautionary tale and I am the mad woman in it,' Chua has said. As a teenager, Lulu gave up playing music and pursued tennis instead. *Don't ruin tennis for me*, she asked of Chua.

At first glance, it may appear that the parent in the trenches with her kid is doing all the hard work, and the lenient ones are just plain lazy. It may seem that the 'tiger mother's' kids are soaring, while others are still playing in the mud, their potential unrealized. The truth is, though, that it is easy to be the 'tiger'. You are the boss, you set the rules, you roar. The little ones get in line—even if it is only because they are temporarily terrorized. It is the 'mother' part that demands courage, as Chua discovered as well. Parents make mistakes, they are vulnerable. They learn to back off and cede territory.

Parents need permission to fail without feeling like failures.

It is a complex web, this parenting. We source the design from deep subconscious wells, from our memory and experience. We repeat patterns from our own childhood. We are the agents of our culture. If Chua decided that her daughters would play musical instruments and excel academically, this was a function of her background—she was the child of Chinese immigrants, in single-minded pursuit of praise, excellence and admiration in America. She had no clue about the value of fun and games.

When Chua asked her fifteen-year-old to suggest a title for her book, the girl said, *The Perfect Child and the Flesh-eating Devil*. Sometimes, it is not so complex after all. Ask a simple question and you might get an answer that will reveal a lot.

Most Indians will recognize the type of tiger mom Chua is. The word love was never used in Chua's childhood home. That sounds familiar, too.

My brothers and I were high-achieving children of strict parents. When I was twelve, I pasted an article in my diary. It was titled, 'The greatest gift you can give your child: self-esteem'. I don't think I knew what self-esteem was, but I must have wanted it badly, because we were not allowed to cut out pages from *Reader's Digest*.

As an adult and a professional coach, I now know that self-confidence is not something anyone can give you to keep forever. It is like a lake in the mountains, a valley of flowers—it must be discovered again and again.

With three young children, we get several opportunities to move gently, stride fiercely, trip and fall. One evening, at my parents' home, when our kids were being kids, I suddenly raised my voice and yelled at them to calm down. I was blunt and fierce. The children were stunned into silence. My father was watching. He will be proud of me, I thought. I'm showing him how well I have learnt to be a strict parent.

Mum called me the next day. 'Your father was saying, "Talk to Natasha. Tell her not to be so harsh, these hurts are not easy to heal. Relax, calm down. Why repeat our mistakes?"'

The voice of Gabbar Singh whispered in my ear, '*Socha tha sardaar khush hoga? Shabaashi dega?*' You thought the boss would be pleased, did you? That he will congratulate you?

I believed my father was the real thing, as far as tiger parents go. And here he was telling me not to be like him. He spoke through Mum, yet something inside me healed. My father was giving me permission to be the change.

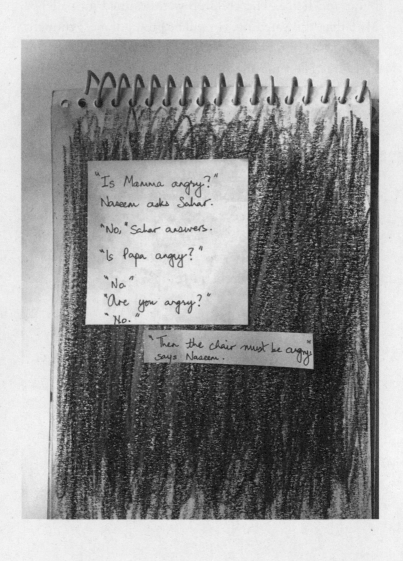

My Daughters' Grandmother

My mother would shake us out of a summer afternoon nap by switching off the fan. I would wake up sweating and miserable, and get out of bed in a terrible mood.

I vowed I would never do this to my children.

Our daughters and I were sitting at the dining table a few weeks ago. We were done with dinner. The house was cool. My husband was travelling. The children were chatting with each other, recalling scenes and dialogues from the animation film they had watched together in the evening.

'Just like this, you will be nineteen, twenty-three and twenty-five, and you will be sitting here chatting and laughing,' I said, with a sense of wonder at how fast children grow up.

'And you will be just the same,' added the youngest child.

'No, Mamma will be older,' said her sister.

'Mamma will be like Nani,' laughed the eldest.

All chit-chat came to an abrupt halt. They looked at me and tried to imagine me like my mother. They shook their heads.

Their grandmother—my mother—is the kindest woman in the world. Her home has the best food. She is energetic and takes them to the park whenever they visit. She has an iPad and two refrigerators full of things that children love. Her afternoon TV shows offer them a dose of forbidden fun. She records *Jhalak Dikhhla Jaa* for them. She has friends with whom she plays tambola in the park. The neighbour's dog visits and creates excitement. Nani never runs out of goldfish crackers and biscuits. The subziwala outside her home gives the children fresh tomatoes and green peas to eat raw. Nani's home is a safe place for everyone she knows.

My children could not imagine me, their crabby and somewhat limited mother, transforming into their multi-talented Nani.

I hadn't realized, until then, that I have competitive feelings when I am compared to my mother. I had always assumed that I was cooler and smarter than her—so the doubts that crept into my children's assessment of me brought me down to earth with a dull thud.

It was a delicious smackdown. 'Try to be more like your mother,' my children were saying to me.

I accepted it.

I am tired of judging my mother. I want to surrender. I want my safe place, too.

Apparently I have taken after my father. I work like him, travel like him and take charge like he does. These are abilities that can be monetized; they are rewarded in a world that values power and achievement outside the home.

Mum gives quietly. If I have it in me to be kind, patient and generous, it is because I have witnessed industrial levels of these qualities in my mother. Generosity is power. Patience is strategy. Kindness is an investment. The ability to defer immediate rewards is life itself.

My mother and I have silent conversations. The less we talk, the more we understand each other. Words have been coming in our way for too many years.

The children and I reached her home one Saturday, after collecting my twelve-year-old's exam results and report card from school. My mother hugged her and asked me about the results.

'She performs very well in class but she didn't seem to apply herself when she was writing her answers,' I quoted her teachers to my mother. 'I wanted to give her more marks,' her teacher had said, 'but she just didn't answer all the questions.'

Even as she continued to hold the child in a cuddle, my mother's expression changed. Her eyes widened as both she and I recognized where we had heard this before.

'Just like you,' said my mother.

'Yes, just like me.'

'It's all right,' she said. 'Children need space. I wish I had more time to spend with you when you were twelve. I was so busy taking care of other people, I missed my own children when they needed me.'

I hugged her, folding her grandchild between her arms and mine. 'Happy Mother's Day,' I whispered.

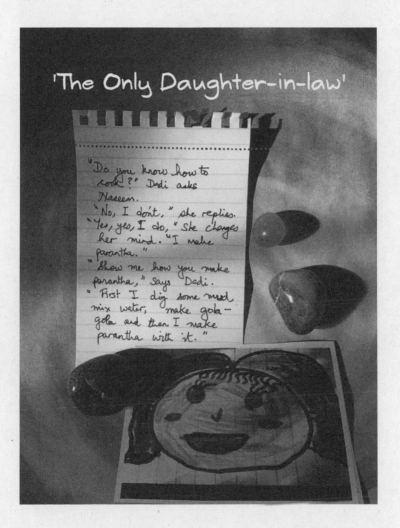

First Meetings and Intangible Longings

My glass bangles clinked. I was in our village in Uttar Pradesh, on a week's break with my family. We were there to celebrate Eid with my husband's extended relations in their home.

It was also our twelfth wedding anniversary. Ammi, my mother-in-law, was hosting a daawat, a feast to celebrate.

'It is your son's wedding anniversary,' I teased her.

'It is also Natasha's anniversary,' she said. 'You are your mother's only daughter and my only daughter-in-law.'

Sarfaraz, a cousin, had brought cake from Varanasi. It was white and yellow and laden with fruits, and when I was ready to cut it, I noticed that my new chikankari kurta had the same colour scheme—the dessert and I matched. Everyone loved the cake, most of all our children, who had been eyeing it suspiciously since it didn't come with the chocolate they were used to.

I felt shy when I thought of this as a wedding anniversary celebration, with the spotlight on my husband and me. This was the first time we were in Ammi's home on this date. I was a bit overwhelmed.

When we first got to know each other and began to spend time together, Afzal and I didn't consider marriage as an option. For years, he was convinced that such a move would hurt his mother very much. We had tested the ground tentatively a few times.

I first met Afzal's parents in a South Indian restaurant

in a Delhi marketplace. The seating had been narrow and tight. No one was sure what to order. I was wearing my crispest cotton suit and a bandhini dupatta to create a good impression. I had acquired a fresh tan on a recent news shoot where my colleague Maya and I had been chasing the Bahujan Samaj Party leader Mayawati during her election campaign in rural Uttar Pradesh. As I got ready to meet Afzal's parents formally, I wore a big maroon bindi on my forehead to soften my face.

In that restaurant, I tried to break the ice with Afzal's father by telling him about my misadventures while trying to get an exclusive interview with Mayawati in Akbarpur. He nodded awkwardly. Ammi was quiet. Afzal's sister walked out with her brother and me into the market corridor to have a chat. I remember thinking that she looked just like Khanna Aunty from Amritsar—the same complexion, body type and that sharp, inquisitive voice.

'Do you think you will be able to adjust to our family?' she asked.

I looked at her blankly, as if this were a scene in a movie and I hadn't had a chance to look at the script.

We abandoned the idea of marrying each other for a long time after this meeting.

When our friends and younger cousins sometimes ask us how we met, Afzal repeats his favourite version of the story. 'Our parents met each other and fixed our marriage and we really had nothing to do with it. I hadn't even seen Natasha before we were married!'

The fact is, many things happened simultaneously and

each event distracted us from the other. It wasn't a bad way to sail through those times. Some episodes carry a haze that I label as 'cultural confusion'. The more we got to know each other's families, the more we discovered how different they were from the version we had reported to each other.

'You know nothing about your mother,' I used to say to my husband. 'She is a love expert!'

He would glow with pride.

I like coming back to this home frequently. I had first visited Afzal's village on a work assignment as a video journalist. We were in the vicinity to film a news feature titled 'Village Voices' and Afzal's family had hosted our three-member crew. When I came back a few years later as a bride who was expected to sit prettily in one place, I imagined myself filming the scene that I was now in the centre of. All these women from the village—those I would have chatted with as a cameraperson—now gawked at me, as I sat quietly, bedecked, trying to look like an old Hindi film heroine while I delicately wiped the sweat off my upper lip. I wanted to get up and sit with the women and crack a joke or two. But I was also enjoying the attention and my role for the moment.

Khem Karan, my father's village on the border by Amritsar, was razed to the ground in a tank war with Pakistan in 1965. My mother's family had left their village near Lahore when they came to Amritsar as refugees after the partition of India in 1947. My grandmother's family abandoned their village home in Makhu, Punjab and came to Delhi after Operation Blue Star in 1984.

I remember feeling greedy about the village I would belong to if and when I married Afzal. It was something I wanted to gift my children. Which is another way of saying I wanted it for myself.

Ammi, the Feminist and Romantic

When our plane landed in Varanasi, the first thing we had to do was switch on our phones and call Ammi. *Ammi, we have landed.* Mothers hate it when they dial your number and your phone is switched off. It triggers a black hole of anxiety in them.

We stopped for dinner on the highway instead of driving straight to our village—it's what Ammi would have wanted. She would have called us many times and told us to eat. *Take a break and get fresh. Make sure the children eat something they like.*

We noted what we ate because she would have asked us for all the details of our meals and snacks. Mothers always want to know what you have eaten.

'I'm glad you ate, but the food must have been terrible,' she would have said.

'No, Ammi, it was quite all right,' I would have answered.

'How can it be? Do you know how they keep their kitchens in these hotels?'

'The *bhindi ki sabzi* was quite nice actually. It looked like a clean place, Ammi.'

'A dhaba on the highway?'

'They can be pretty decent, Ammi. You only asked us to eat on the way.'

'That's how you pick up stomach bugs when you visit.'

'Ammi, last time I got a stomach infection after the big feast in the haveli in Ghazipur . . .'

'Agree with your mother-in-law,' my teacher, Father Os had told me in one of his group therapy sessions.

'What?'

'Just agree with whatever she says.'

'How can I do that, Father Os? She says contrary things.'

'Just agree with her,' he had said. 'Try it. You won't cease to exist.'

'How was the food?' Ammi had asked soon after.

'It was quite all right, Ammi.'

'It must have been terrible.'

'Yes actually, the rotis were like leather and the bhindi was dripping with oil.'

'What did you expect? It can't be like home food.'

'That's true.'

'They do the best they can.'

'True, Ammi.'

'You are too delicate.'

'That's true,' I smiled.

'You can get a stomach bug from eating at home, too.'

'That's also true. Last time I did!'

'I'm glad you ate and I am glad you are coming home.'

Ammi laughed. The smallest of things made Ammi laugh—like her daughter-in-law unexpectedly agreeing with her, or the sight of a baby—anyone's baby.

On the way to the airport, I had turned to my children and said, 'Ammi was one of the nicest mothers ever.'

They nodded solemnly.

'Your father is a very lucky man. And we are very lucky, too.'

Just that morning, I had read Sohaila Abdulali's column in *Mint Lounge*, in which she recalled that it had been almost six years since her father had died. Six years of being a person with a dead father. She called it 'good grief'—being buoyed by the memories of the good times they had had together.

I went up to Afzal and read the article out to him. He held back tears as he listened. We are all preparing ourselves for the inevitability of the death of our parents.

He had called his mother right after I had placed down the newspaper. She had said she was feeling drowsy. She wanted to change the medication she was on. Three hours later, Afzal's sister called and told him that Ammi had fallen asleep and passed on. Their mother was dead. Our Ammi was no more.

Afzal handed his phone to me and asked me to take all calls. He went to his room to pray. 'Tell my friends to call me a week later.'

I dialled my mother's number. I texted my brothers. Our children were having lunch. They got up and started crying spontaneously. I held them close.

'You are Piku,' I had told Afzal, after we had recently watched the Shoojit Sircar movie. 'You are always driving cross-country with or for your parents. And discussing their ablutions.'

I stepped forward and held Ammi's hand when her body was being prepared for burial. It was soft, as usual. She had asked Noorie to create a mehndi pattern on her palm. She hadn't done that for years. The dark beauty of the henna design was startling.

Ammi's small hands, white with blue veins, balancing a large papaya or watermelon as she sliced it neatly at the breakfast table. Why do we remember our parents' hands so much? The hands that had held us when we were babies—balancing our bottoms in those palms as we grew into independence.

'Your daughter-in-law seems like she is your daughter. No one can tell that there is a new bahu in this house,' Ammi's neighbour had once commented. It was meant to be a taunt.

'That sounds like a good thing,' Ammi had answered.

She repeated it to me later. 'People say that my daughter-in-law doesn't behave like a bahu, and I tell them that's how I want it. This is your home. Everything here belongs to you now.'

Here I was behaving like a daughter all over again—sitting by her bed, typing snippets into my phone, while others handled the logistical details of her burial.

'Your mother is a feminist,' I have often said to Afzal.

He used to be terrified that there would be nothing in common between his mother and me.

Ammi negotiated complex patriarchal systems every day. And she ruled. She was not afraid of being unpopular. She took charge and got things done. She spoke her mind fearlessly, sometimes sounding very harsh. She loved openly and with confidence. Ammi was a romantic. She recognized love when she saw it. She protected us. 'There's no way you and I would have survived together on our own,' I'd tell Afzal.

As I watched her body, I knew she would have given me

a copy of the Quran in English to read with everyone else. I don't know where she keeps it.

I don't even need it this time. Writing about her is my prayer. It soothes me. It keeps her alive for me.

She would also have sent me a glass of chocolate milk. She was alert to everyone's needs. How do mothers do that?

We ache to belong to places. It is always people who make us belong. When they are gone, the place doesn't recognize us any more. We have to build relationships from scratch again.

Ammi and I both love the same man. This is our bond of solidarity. Her family is my family.

Ammi was the home I was trying to give my children. She is the wellspring at which we replenish ourselves.

Looking Out for Papa

Growing up means that there isn't always time to pause when you need to cry desperately. You learn to postpone tears. The tears get stored up and come at unexpected moments. Safe moments. I welled up at an award ceremony recently and a friend who saw me from the stage sent me a text message to ask what was wrong. Through my tears, I smiled at the thought that he was both hosting the show and sending texts to people in the front row. 'You multitask like a woman,' I was tempted to bait him, but I didn't.

'Just pent-up tears,' I texted back, hoping to make sense.

I went home to meet my mother on my way back from work one day and told her that I had come to cry.

'Can't cry at home,' I told her. 'No time, no space.'

She seemed to understand. She fed me first. Food that I once used to find ordinary is now the most reassuring, nurturing taste in the world for me.

'You don't get old and die, okay,' I said to her.

'Of course I will,' she whispered, almost laughing. 'Beta, this is going to happen to everyone.' She was so calm about it—as though it were a great new phase to look forward to. Her serenity pacified me.

At home, my husband and I are taking care of his father as he recovers from a spinal fracture and other assorted age-related illnesses. Over two months, we have become mini-experts—visiting specialists, reading online, balancing alternative and mainstream therapies, listening to everyone and taking decisions with our fingers crossed.

While we juggle hospitals, school and work schedules, our lives are being micro-managed by Kanta and Taslimun at home. Often we hear peals of laughter as the women bond over tea and shared stories from each other's families and villages.

It amuses me that most of Papa's super-specialized doctors are either my age or younger. I hadn't quite noticed before that the world around us has got much younger than us.

Despite his discomfort, Papa is a model patient. Even when he is extremely irritated, his language remains polite. As soon as his pain subsides, he jokes with us, completely putting everyone at ease. He obsesses over everyone's schedules, reminding us about all the appointments and commitments of the day.

Then there are Papa's visitors. It's as though a whole cross-section of India is walking in and out of our home, pausing to advise Papa and us in their own unique way. As we host visitors who come from far away, our home becomes a hub of get-togethers. There are poets and politicians, family and other well-wishers. Papa misses being in our village in Ghazipur, and a house full of people reassures him.

Despite your reluctance, you are well on the way to becoming the family matriarch, I laugh at myself. I send photos of Papa to all his children—Papa drinking tea from a cup without assistance; Papa sitting outside in the courtyard in the evening; Papa at the dining table with everyone. It may last for twenty minutes but each milestone asks to be celebrated.

The outside world continues to bring in its regular doses of tragic news—photographs of a bloodied man begging for his life before he is lynched in the presence of policemen in Jharkhand; a bomb blast at a concert in Manchester. Even though his eye infection is healed and he has new glasses, Papa refuses to resume reading the newspapers.

In the midst of it all, our daughters left for week-long school trips. We patted ourselves on the back for the minor achievement of being able to drop them off on time to catch their early morning Shatabdi train with their schoolmates.

I have pulled out my copy of Elisabeth Kübler-Ross' memoir *The Wheel of Life*, and carry it everywhere with me. I read it when I am waiting outside the physiotherapy room in the hospital where Papa is learning to get back on his feet again. Within weeks, he has moved from being on the stretcher, to the wheelchair, to using a walker for support.

'Life ends when you have learned everything you are supposed to learn,' wrote Kübler-Ross as she tried to find meaning in the suffering her mother endured when she was paralysed in the last few years of her life.

Chapter Thirty in Kübler-Ross' memoir of living and dying is titled 'Death Does Not Exist'. Just the heading consoles me. I have announced to my family that for my birthday, I want all of Kübler-Ross' other books—especially her ground-breaking *On Death and Dying*, in which she first talked about the five stages of grief.

This stage in our adult life when we are the parents of young children and the children of ageing parents is fascinating. As we slip from one role into another, we often find ourselves entirely stressed out and exhausted. But I must admit that I also feel calm and in control. I feel important. It's a privilege and I am grateful.

Last week, Papa's son decided to resume work-related travel.

'Papa, who would you rather have in charge? Should I give the responsibility of taking care of your needs to Natasha—or to your granddaughter Naseem?' he asked Papa.

'You are asking me as if there is a difference between Naseem and Natasha,' said Papa in his slow morning voice. 'Naseem is Natasha and Natasha is Naseem.'

'Yay for Papa,' I said, marvelling at his wisdom. This is really all I need to keep going. One line at a time that hits the bullseye.

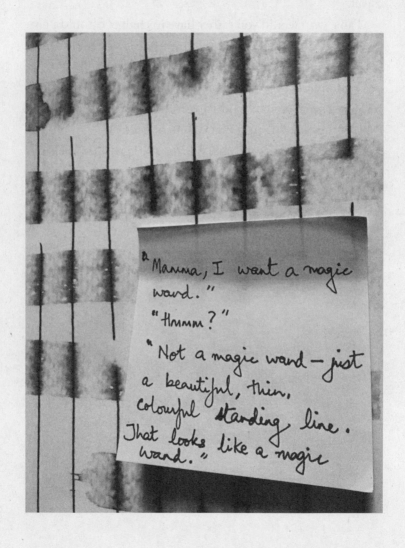

Heaven Is Where the Fruit Trees Are

Ammi loved trees. She talked about them the way many of us love and speak about our pets.

The first thing I noticed about Ammi's home when I began to visit her regularly was that it faced both ways. There was no 'back'. On one side, we would park the car and enter the home, and on the other side, we would sit, read, play and eat, facing the garden. I haven't yet found an English word for a lawn that is towards the rear of a house—in Urdu it is called a 'haata'.

Ammi spent her day in the inner courtyard, looking out at the birds, flowering shrubs and fruits—the mango, papaya and pomegranate trees. Occasionally, a langur would visit and cause some excitement. There were vegetable patches, lemon trees and a fragrant mehndi plant. The tallest and most majestic was a jamun tree.

A few days after Ammi died, I went up to her garden to feel her presence. It had been raining and the jamun tree was laden with ripe fruit. We organized the children in the house and got Muzammil to shake the upper branches with a bamboo stick. It rained jamuns all around us. They were voluptuous in our mouths. I wrote about the jamun tree. I took photos of it. It was a celebration of life.

Later, I was at the dining table with six-year-old Naseem.

'Will you die before me, Mamma?' she asked me.

'Yes, Naseem,' I said.

'Will you be there when I reach heaven?'

'Yes, I will.'

'Will you tell god that I really like jamun?'

'Yes.'

'Then he can make sure there is always some jamun for me,' she said, putting another one in her mouth.

Keep it simple, I said to myself, taking a cue from the child.

Shazi, my friend, sent me an email with a photo of a sunflower from her garden in Canada. Sunflowers seem like people to me. Tall, with expressive faces, always commenting on the weather and waving at everyone who passes by.

'You know, sometimes I wonder—how do people cope with the death of a loved one without a bit of faith in the world after and the power of prayer?' Shazi wrote to me. 'Prayer and faith help me in difficult times, in times of sorrow and grief.'

'I wish I were more religious,' said another friend, Sabrina, whose husband, Steve, had died suddenly. 'I can't bring myself to believe in an afterlife. People tell me to imagine him looking out for our son and me. I feel that if Steve can really see us, he must be miserable, because there is nowhere he'd want to be except with his son.'

I read them and wondered if I was religious. I don't really pray in any formal way. I don't fast or read religious texts. But I believe. I have faith.

I'm thinking of my mother a lot. For years, when she would recall her parents and the homes in which she grew up, I could barely connect with her stories. Now I do. She needs to remember where she comes from to feel alive in her present.

Aliza was ten years old when Ammi had died. When we returned home after Ammi's last rites, Aliza went to school for a day and then refused to go again. She was not ill. She would wake up agitated and remain that way till we agreed to let her stay at home. After that, Aliza would be perfectly fine and well-adjusted for the day. She'd stay close to me, and go wherever I·went. One day, she sat with her books and colours in a corner of a conference room throughout a five-hour work meeting. Another day, she accompanied a friend and me to shops, tagging along quietly and patiently.

On the fourth day of missing school, Aliza asked me if I knew why she couldn't bring herself to go back. I had a clue. Everything was so normal in school. Aliza was hurting. She needed permission and space to grieve.

We were experiencing the same thing. When we were in spaces where we could talk about Ammi and her death, we felt better than when we were out there in the world where it didn't matter. We sought conversation with people who knew her essential self. There'd be a time to move on. We'd know when it would come.

My Husband's Wife

"What are you writing?" he asks me.

"How to resurrect love from the ruins of a marriage overrun by children," I say.

"That's audacious!" he laughs.

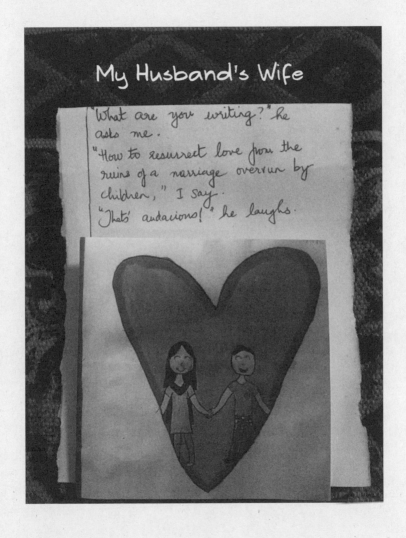

Five Things to Learn from the Spouse

Often, my husband and I look at each other and wonder afresh what a sterling person like him/me is doing with a strange person like me/him. Let me simplify this.

I am sterling and he is strange and this is what he believes, too—not that he is strange and I am sterling—he believes the opposite.

But if you look at it in a certain way, we both believe exactly the same thing. That the other has got a much better deal than the self.

So, we are on the same page. Except for the very rare moments when he thinks about me and feels an overwhelming urge to thank god for his amazing luck. Not god's luck, his own luck. But this is rare. It is so rare that it almost never happens.

They used to try to convince us that marriage is primarily a transaction between families. It is not something that individuals like the bride and groom are supposed to take too personally. Of course, we rebelled against the outdated idea—and then we learnt that it wasn't *that* off the mark either.

In so many ways, we find that most conflicts between us amount to the differences between the boy his parents have raised and the girl my parents have raised.

Every time we reach a point where we just can't believe how the other can be so daft/insensitive/hurtful, all we have to do is back off and remember how different the idea of 'everyday normal' is in the families we grew up in. Consciously or otherwise, we feel compelled to recreate the same 'normal' in the families we build as adults. His normal and my normal come face to face with each other every day, convinced that the other is really *very* abnormal indeed.

I'm here to admit that my husband, like most husbands, is a well-loved spoilt brat. I am also here to admit that I have secretly been taking notes and this is the very first list of things that I have gleaned by watching him surreptitiously, while he thought I was immersed in work or daily social media duties.

Learn to fight

In the beginning I used to believe that my role in a conflict was to be the quiet, wise one—the one whose precious tears would roll silently down her pretty face and the one who would be consoled later with hugs and an apology. This idea got me into a lot of trouble with my beloved because he is no good at interpreting silence, and the sight of tears sets off all the wrong triggers in him. But, now, I have caught on! I have learnt from my husband to enter headlong into arguments, raise my voice and say what comes to my mind in long-winded sentences . . . and stop only when I need to catch my breath. This is fun. And, most of the time, it works!

Learn to feel at home

My husband is a vagabond just like me, but unlike me he seems to find a home everywhere. I, on the other hand, can feel like an outsider even in my own skin. I used to feel sorry for my husband—for how deluded he was being—till I calmed down and realized that it is okay to calm down. It is okay to belong. Fitting in once in a while really doesn't hurt at all. Often, you get very nice things to eat.

Learn not to be offended

I really don't know what kind of cauldron this man, who is my husband, fell into as a child. Perhaps it is because he spends extraordinarily little time surfing the Internet—but my husband knows next to nothing about the things one is supposed to be offended or outraged by. He often mistakes insults for genuine interest.

'Why don't you go to Pakistan?' someone will yell at him in the middle of a parking argument in the peak of Delhi's summer. Of course, the stranger is reacting to the information he has just gathered—that my husband's name is Afzal.

'I would gladly go to Pakistan,' Afzal will reply, 'but I really want to go to Mohenjo-daro and they'll never grant me a visa for that. Who wants to be stuck in Karachi, having late night dinners with relatives, you know what I mean?'

Learn to be a gracious host

Afzal is always inviting people over and making place for unexpected invaders—I mean guests—without ever worrying about what we will feed them or where they will sleep. When I look like I have been struck by lightning, he will say, 'Natasha, they have come to meet us! Stop being silly about food and beds. Logistics is never a challenge. Just be good company.'

Over the years, I have finally stopped believing that people drop in to judge me or get served by me. I present mashed spinach and chopped cabbage on the table as happily as he does, and when they ask if someone in our family is ill, I smile sweetly at them, as Afzal takes over and lectures them on healthy eating habits.

Drink tea and do nothing

At first, it is very hard. It is difficult not to participate in urgent global crises by updating your Facebook status. It is hard not to sort laundry and rearrange shoe racks in the house. Then you get better at it. You fleetingly think about all the things that need to be done and do zilch about any of them.

There is nothing like having a role model at home to learn life skills from, and if you are as sterling as I am and have fallen in love with a strange person (this is the only way love works, actually), I hope you are using every opportunity you get to beat the strange person at his own game by learning his repertoire of tricks while he is busy drinking tea and doing nothing.

My Husband Is Not Fond of Husbands

My husband is an expert on husbands. He spots 'husband behaviour' immediately and points it out to me.

'You are behaving like the husband,' he tells me when we sit with family or friends and I pick up my phone and start scrolling through notifications. I put my phone away—unless I happen to be booking a ticket for him on the Indian railways website, in which case, I win.

I tell him a dirty joke. After smiling shyly and blushing, he recovers his wits and says to me, 'See, I told you, you are the husband in this relationship.'

'You think wives don't tell dirty jokes?'

'I don't know any,' he admits.

'Well, you had better not know any,' I say. 'I don't want other people's wives telling you dirty jokes.'

He blushes again.

He makes the beds on the berths of trains, carefully tucking in the sheets and hoisting each one of us so the sheets don't slip off at night. He remakes the beds at home to get the lines just right on all sides—like his mother taught him to.

I used to rinse and organize the dirty dishes neatly in the kitchen sink before the maid would come and wash them. After we had three children and I began to work from home, I let the dishes pile up and scatter across the kitchen counter. I allowed the beds to remain undone all day. I couldn't keep up with the underwear requirements of each member of the family. I let the children wear unironed shirts to school.

The last time I was travelling for work, my husband took the children to the supermarket and bought each of them individual hairbrushes. He discovered that everyone's school socks were collapsing around the ankles and rectified the situation.

'You work like a man,' he said to me. 'You work more than men. You work twenty-four hours a day.' He was spotting husband-behaviour again.

My husband is not fond of husbands.

'I miss you too, jaanoo,' I sometimes have the presence of mind to say. He is not complaining, he is just missing me.

Lately, I have also started pointing things out.

I name his sisters and say, 'Your favourite women are also at work almost all their waking hours. But because they do housework and host guests and take on their children's, husband's and in-law's work, no one accuses them of working too much. In fact, no one notices that they work at all.

'The difference between them and me is that I choose the work I do.'

This is an important conversation—not only because we want to avoid nagging and diminishing each other, but also because we are raising children together. Notably, daughters. We know that they will confront social attitudes that aim to restrict their life choices. They will be told: You are intimidating if you are smart; you are unsexy if you are funny; you are attractive only if you remain demure at work, on stage, while presenting, while receiving, while grieving, while laughing, while birthing.

This would have been an equally important conversation if we had been raising sons. Boys don't need to be caged in by restrictive notions of gender-appropriate behaviour either.

'Both of you are being so sensitive,' our daughter interjects at the dinner table, making us withdraw from yet another argument that we didn't even realize we had begun having. Every child deserves to grow up in an environment that he or she is allowed to question and examine intimately. Every child needs to experience that love is not a cage.

I have, over a period of time, come to realize that a good marriage is a terrible burden. Our desperation to keep up appearances forces us to look away from things that might be bothering us. Silence perpetuates fear and infantilizes us. It makes us lazy. We return home carrying unexpressed anger and dump the discontentment in our safe place.

This confuses the hell out of the children.

True love involves a lot of fighting. It involves letting go of fights, too.

It is okay to let our marriage look a little bit bad.

I have learnt to take on others in the world by watching my husband. Every time I come to him with a story about how badly I have been treated by someone, he compels me to get out of the position of a victim. He is horrible. He supports the other. He forces me to recover words to defend my position. I struggle to clarify, explain and examine my own feelings. I am forced to accept my role in the conflict I have brought back home with me.

Inevitably, I practise my newly acquired skills on him.

Marriage is a boxing ring. Have I used this metaphor before?

Ready to Celebrate Our Differences

A good long day had been folded and put away for the night—and suddenly, there was an unexpected argument.

I forget what the disagreement was about, but I remember its trajectory. A casual remark sparked a more vehement assertion from one of us. My tone became sharp. His voice grew loud. It felt like he was yelling at me. I was ready to back off, but by now he was on a roll.

I looked at the child who was watching us. I hoped that he would see that both our child and I were distraught. I held her in my arms and lay down with her to sleep. I wanted to reassure her that it was just a temporary fight; that arguments are a part of life; that we'd sort it out tomorrow.

I slept through the night instead of lying awake like my younger self would have. It was a milestone in our relationship—that I could turn away from an unfinished fight and just fall asleep.

The next morning demanded its own rhythm. There were children to get ready for school. There was the bus-stop-and-breakfast routine. He emerged. He was sorry but he wouldn't say he was sorry. He sat looking sorry. Some tears rolled down my cheeks. We distracted each other by talking about logistics, and other people, and future plans. Then we settled into quiet. He still wouldn't say sorry.

It might have been a good idea to just apologize and get on with life.

But we are not efficient. Love is not efficient. It slows

us down. Marriage chugs along, getting the work done. It has other deadlines to meet.

We used to be the annoying couple who never seemed to disagree with each other. Friends would mock us for being so well behaved.

When my husband and I exchanged gifts on our tenth wedding anniversary, I asked him for a few good arguments. I want to let go of the silences, I said. Afzal would get angry and give up, mid-way, the messy task of confrontation. I would get nervous and deny the existence of any conflict. One reason why we seemed to get along so well was the fear that we had very little in common.

In the eleventh year, we learned to fight. By the end of that year, I was ready celebrate our differences.

I am really good at making money and Afzal is really good at spending it. 'You are not supposed to keep money,' he reminds me, 'you are supposed to spend it on what you want.' I don't get his logic at all. What are bank accounts for? What are fixed deposits for? What are envelopes stashed between saris in the cupboard for? Before I had children, I was saving for their school fees. Now, I must save for their higher education, no?

Apparently not.

Between my husband and me, I am learning to spend money after I have earned it and he is learning to earn money before he spends it.

For the most part, while growing up, we were a nuclear family, living in small apartments in big cities. His home is a large, extended family living in a sprawling haveli in his village. He opens doors and windows, no matter where he is, to let in fresh air. I am learning to live with dust everywhere. I grow indoor plants in cracked coffee mugs. He plants trees that will bring fruit, birds and shade for all. He is beginning to share my joy on witnessing the tight fist of a new leaf by the windowsill. I pretend to be interested when he gushes about the trees that will surround us a decade from now. We live on the edge, between my city and his village.

When setting food on the table, I use the words 'practical' and 'logic' a lot. He talks of *adaab-e-dastarkhwan*–the etiquette of the dining table. I get impressed and accept his version of table etiquette. Besides, he's in charge of the rules he sets.

We have the compulsive habit of showing each other the mirror. There was a time when I would come home, enamoured by the CEO I worked with, and narrate anecdotes in awe. 'The property dealers I meet are better than these corporate honchos,' he'd respond. 'Whatever they are, they are on the outside. They are honest that way.'

We are outsiders in each other's worlds. We make one another very uncomfortable in what is meant to be our comfort zone. Sometimes, it gets to be too much and we fight. Then, we redefine and articulate our choices again.

Marriage is the bad cop who keeps us on our toes. Love is the good cop who announces tea breaks.

'Stop analyzing everything, Natasha,' my husband tells me. 'Life is not for analyzing, it is for living. Live it.'

'Okay,' I respond.

'Why are you so quiet?' he asks me after a long pause.

'You said, "No analysis". I am being obedient.'

His face crinkles up in amusement.

Finding a Cure in Love

The thing with being in the troubled waters of love is that there is always a bright side.

One of the lessons I have learnt over the years is that we can love each other deeply and still not understand anything much about one another. This is slightly better than understanding each other deeply and not feeling any love.

We can talk a lot and discover years later that we need to learn to hear each other. To make love work we need to make our emotions work for us, rather than against us.

My husband, Afzal, had been travelling for a while and he brought this up with me a few days after returning home: 'I saw that you stopped taking your Tibetan medicines and even wrote about it!'

'Yes,' I admitted sheepishly.

'I read it. You sounded like you were bragging that you didn't want to be healthy.'

'Maybe it was a cry for help,' I answered in a small voice.

Afzal wants me to address the niggling ailments that come and go all the time—like bruxism, or errant stomach aches, or recurring eczema patches. If stress makes me ill, he wants me to confront my stress. I, on the other hand, suffer the symptoms and then forget about fixing them—till they return and seriously get in my way again.

He brought this up with our Tibetan doctor when we visited her next.

'Let her be, she seems healthy,' said the doctor. 'I can do without her money,' she joked.

In response, I dutifully offered a list of disconnected symptoms.

Our Tibetan doctor is the mother of two grown-up daughters. She looked at my husband and said, 'I think she needs to work. Let her go to an office.'

Afzal's eyes became dinner plates. 'Work?' he responded. 'She works twelve hours, no, eighteen hours, no, twenty-two hours a day! Maybe she needs to work a little less.'

'Uh, okay,' said the doctor. 'Don't stop her from doing anything.'

'I don't do that,' said Afzal. 'I mean, I have no right to do that.'

As for me, I enjoyed myself so thoroughly—as two adults discussed my ailments and the ideal cure—that I didn't mind the idea of taking Tibetan medicines four times a day now.

Love and intimacy are at the root of all that makes us sick and well, wrote Dean Ornish in his book *Love and Survival*.

One day, I read Steve Paulson's interview of literary theorist Gayatri Chakravorty Spivak online. It was full of insights. I saved it to read out an excerpt to Afzal. Spivak said:

> That's what deconstruction is about, right? It's not just destruction. It's also construction. It's critical intimacy, not critical distance [. . .] My teacher Paul de Man once said to another very great critic, Fredric Jameson, 'Fred, you can only deconstruct what you love.' Because you are doing it from the inside, with real intimacy.

I felt that perhaps this explained my constant urge to examine and write about my most intimate relationships. It also explained my relative reluctance to write about others, which should have come naturally to me as a journalist.

'This is why I keep talking about the same thing,' I said by way of explanation.

For Afzal, Spivak's words became a weapon for the future. For days afterwards, every time he wanted to analyze or 'deconstruct' me, he would start like this: 'It is because I have critical intimacy with you and I love you that I am saying this to you . . .'

It ceased to matter what he wished to say next. Here was the man who used to argue in our early years together that saying 'I love you' was phoney. 'People who keep repeating "I love you" are the ones who mean it the least. Those who are really in love don't need to say it,' he would assert. Yet, an extract from a Gayatri Spivak interview seemed to have transformed the man. Either that, or he had plain forgotten his early impressions about the true expression of love.

Recently, when he wanted to confront me about not having a structure to my day and being addicted to the rush and anxiety of deadlines, he chose to start with, 'I love you and that is why I am saying this, but you must deconstruct your laziness . . .' Or something to that effect.

Like I said, it didn't matter what he said after he spoke the first three words. I got what I needed.

I like critical intimacy, it has such a nice ring to it.

'Mamma, is it Kanta Mausi's birthday on Saturday?'

'No, beta, it is Karwa Chauth. She will wear new clothes and bangles.'

'What is Karwa Chauth?' asks Aliza.

'It is a day to celebrate husbands,' I say.

'Husbands? How?' asks Naseem.

'Wives don't eat anything for the whole day. They wear new clothes and put mehndi on their palms.'

'But... if Mammas don't eat anything, how will they grow up?' asks Naseem.

'But Papa doesn't eat for a whole month in Ramzan,' says Aliza. 'They are already grown up.'

'Mamma, will you not eat?' Naseem asks.

'I will, jaanoo,' I say.

'You will celebrate him... in other ways?'

'Yes, I will.'

They are satisfied.

Making Sense of a Four-letter Word

Love is an empty house you move into.

Love isn't always a good home.

Homes have dark corners, awkward spaces and places you are just not willing to go to for reasons you cannot fathom. Homes can stay unfamiliar for years. So can love.

When we move in with love, it changes its colours.

In the beginning, we like love to look good. We assume that if we make it appear great, it will *be* great. When that doesn't happen, it feels like a dark, heavy secret.

Love is a laggard. It doesn't always turn up on stage according to script. It goes missing, leaving the rest of the actors to improvise awkwardly.

Love doesn't do its homework. Love procrastinates. Love goes off to pick up its phone in the middle of a conversation. Love sneaks a look at its mobile notifications, as soon as it sees you approaching. How much love does love need? Love is an ungrateful, entitled brat.

Love likes togetherness. Love underestimates how much space it seeks. It needs bus rides and highways. It needs distance to sustain itself. It needs to breathe, to run, to go away, so it can return to safe embraces.

The truth is, love can be aloof. Love doesn't always know how to be intimate. You may hug it and hold it tight, but it forgets that it needs to shift on the bench and make space for you. Your allegiance can stay one-sided for years.

~

In our personal spaces, some of us are threatened by the love we feel. We resent the fact that we don't feel love like we expected ourselves to. What is wrong with us?

Love means dealing with differences. Accepting contradictions. Learning to listen without relying on words.

In love, you become the keeper of each other's memories. He will tell you about the uncle who bullied him—and then forget about it, leaving you to deal with the offensive man when he comes visiting. He will tell you about crushes and heartbreaks. You will tell him about the trees in your childhood home and the cake your mother used to bake on birthdays. Love is a repository of childhood stories.

One of you will be the dreamer. The other will be fantastic with logistics. One will assume charge of getting all the details right. The other will ask, 'Why are we always late everywhere?' One of you will write deeply embarrassing Facebook posts. The other will be a WhatsApp enthusiast. One will thrive in clutter. The other will always wipe the bathroom floor dry. One of you will get along fine with plumbers, electricians, carpenters and subziwalas. The other will be an intolerable, ill-mannered, defensive, lazy fool. Both will frustrate each other. Love makes us weary.

One of you will be better at waking up the children kindly, and tucking them into bed at night. It will take years to realize that roles can be switched. It's quite simple.

You will develop a good-cop-bad-cop reputation without realizing it. It will hurt when you discover that one of you is always viewed as hateful, while the other wears a halo.

Remember to reverse your positions in time. Don't wait for the other's permission.

In love, you will learn to ask each other for money—you will be angry and disappointed and afraid. One of you will have a healthier relationship than the other with finances. You may love money by spending it; he may love it by keeping it close. Money is the third party in your romance.

When in love, you will trust each other. When in love, you will be suspicious. This will stun you. Step back. Trust has to be earned. One of you will have trust issues.

In love, you will watch each other fight losing battles. You will want to rescue the other from obsessions. You will be judgemental. You will tear each other down. You will bask in reflected glory when the other wins. You will feel left out. Love makes us uncomfortable.

Love demands patience. He may be no good at being ill. He may get cranky and hyperactive, refusing to admit that all he needs is rest. He may have no clue about how to deal with you when *you* are ill. He will keep forgetting that you are in pain. Instead of being gentle, he will yell at you when he discovers the medicines you have stashed away, long after you were supposed to have taken them.

Your weakness triggers anxiety in the lover. It makes him feel vulnerable—and vulnerability must be stomped. A simple fever becomes a raging volcano rumbling beneath a household. You take it personally. How can you not?

Love takes years to get comfortable in its skin. Love has childhood issues.

~

Now, put everything back in a box and shake it till the bones rattle. The doctor recommends a good shake-up in her prescription for love.

The most significant phase of marriage and love is when the two of you become separate persons again—with your own rhythm, priorities, angst, pleasures and passions; with your separate dreams to fulfil. It is scary. You will wonder if the love is over.

True love wants the lover to be truly liberated. True love has abandonment anxiety.

True love can be healed. It reinvents itself. It revives.

Love demands diversification. Love more, love others, love in new ways. Rediscover kissing in new places. Find new destinations for yourselves to keep your love alive.

Love is a decision—a choice you make again and again.

The Workplace Goer

"Mamma, are you going for a party?"
asks Naseem, touching my clothes
"No baby, I am going to office.
"Thats' what I meant, she says.

How to Have It All

This is somewhat embarrassing to admit—but I have the feeling that I have it all.

I typed this really quickly because although I have been sensing it for a while now, it seems like a rude or inappropriate thing to say. I don't mean to be a show-off.

The more I read and hear about women and their conflicts at workplaces, with motherhood and childcare choices, the more I long to hear a version that will make me raise my hand and say, 'Yes, that's my story, too.'

But nothing fits.

I toy with the idea that either I don't understand what everyone else is saying or I don't understand myself yet. But no—that isn't true.

So, let me put it out there—why I feel I have it all.

First, the glorious relationship I have had with my full-time job. Not my work, my job.

As a woman who joined the television industry in the mid-1990s, I started as a video journalist—the first woman to be a news cameraperson in India. It was really a love affair between a young urban woman and her workplace. My job at New Delhi Television offered a buffer from my family; it was a runaway joint that let me escape the rollercoaster ride of the twenties and thirties; most importantly, it was the shell that held me together as I constructed an independent sense of my own self.

When I first joined the office, I gave myself a year there.

I did some elementary calculations. It seemed like working for one year would enable me to save enough money to support myself and spend the next year doing whatever I wanted to without needing a salary. At the end of the first year, I realized my calculations had not been very accurate. Plus, I was loving being a working professional. There was so much to learn, do and experience. I gave myself another year. Then another. And another. It was love all right. The travel, the journalism and honing the craft of videography was an immense privilege. Returning to office after work trips was like coming home. We were growing together. When fatigue began to set in, I took a six-month sabbatical. When I needed more time to complete a teaching project I had started, I sent a heartfelt note to my employers Radhika and Prannoy Roy.

'My office is my playground,' I wrote. In any other industry, this might have been a horrifyingly unprofessional confession, but in our office, at that time, it was a compliment. I got extra leave to complete the year-long media access course I had started teaching in Bhilai, Chhattisgarh.

I changed roles within the same workplace. I re-trained and switched departments. Like many others, I quickly and steadily rose within the ranks.

Then, as soón as I began to peak as a professional, I quit. I was vice president, training and development. I had a shiny visiting card, an office car and a glass cubicle at work.

'Ah, you quit work because of the children,' people would nod with a look of obvious understanding.

'No, because of me,' I would reply. 'I didn't quit work, I quit my full-time job. I'm still working . . .'

But no one was listening.

I was the mother of little children. We had excellent childcare facilities at my workplace. My role allowed me to work from home when I needed to. My appraisals, promotions and benefits had been soaring higher than ever before. I loved my smartphone. My wardrobe was full of sharp business suits and a range of footwear I referred to as 'airport shoes'.

'I want to stop because I have never stopped and I am exhausted. And I am fulfilled as well,' I wrote in an email to a friend. I was standing by a street corner in Manhattan tapping these words with a stylus into my phone. A pocket of sunlight, the distance from home and the solitude of a free morning during a work trip suddenly brought some things into perspective for me. 'Other Natashas, the ones who write, nap during the day, cycle to the gym, cook a meal, I want to let those Natashas out.'

I missed my children. I wanted to know the guy I had married. I wanted to be with myself. It was time to remove the scaffolding of my job and inaugurate a new life. So, I quit for love.

Love's a decent hobby—but can you make a vocation out of it? Maybe you can. What about a calling? Motherhood could be my calling.

Who knows what is around the corner till we turn it? Who is to tell what is inside us till we stand still and let it emerge?

For a long time, I mourned the loss of my job. I wrote a poetic email to my bosses as I watched the sun set into the Mediterranean Sea over a holiday in Sardinia. My husband was embarrassed for me. 'Why are you doing this?' he asked.

I was sure I wanted to do it. I was letting go of a love and I longed to express that. I was enunciating my deep admiration for the people I had grown up with. People who had believed in me, enabling me to believe in myself. These had been the best years of my life.

One way to have it all is to agree to not want everything together at all times. Besides, having-it-all is a feeling, not a comparative analysis. I was ready to do something new. I didn't know what that was. But I knew what I didn't want to keep on doing. I gave myself permission to enter unchartered territory. The way would reveal itself.

Exeunt Office

I told a friend that a straightforward, honest sequel to the 'How to have it all' essay would be one titled 'I miss the money'.

Let me confess: I do. I also miss the glamour and the casual self-importance of a ten-hour workday. I miss the easy sense of power. I miss having a one-line bio. I feel the loss of a visiting card—of the supportive framework of an official designation and a pass with a logo that opens doors everywhere.

Was it easy quitting my job? Hardly. It was like having a baby. They tell you it is perfectly natural, but everything feels strange. There is pain. It takes aeons for things to settle.

In the early days, it felt as if I had returned a borrowed superhero's costume and walked into the street in everyday clothes, like a nobody.

Admittedly, my superhero life had developed some chinks. I had begun to notice that on the commute between work and home, I would sit by the edge of the seat in my car, instead of relaxing or putting up my feet. The urgency of con-calls that got us nowhere confused me. My dentist told me that I was grinding my teeth in my sleep.

Taking tough decisions is only the first step; it's when the decisions move in with us and overstay their welcome that the party really begins.

I came home. I hated being home. We were a mess, both the home and I. I yelled at maids, I disliked everyone who rang the doorbell. I made a few good salads. I missed fully air conditioned interiors. I didn't know what I did any more.

Being at the bus stop to receive my children was no longer a novelty. The enthusiasm I would display was feigned. And the children knew it. It is supposed to be the most uncomplicated of our loves—our love for our children. It is also the most vulnerable.

I read an email from a reader named Ritu—she listed everything she had achieved and wondered why she was still unhappy. She thought she would feel liberated when she quit her job and could own her own time, but 'in the last five years of having left the job, I have barely been to shopping malls or to a beauty parlour—no more than I was doing before.'

I wrote back to her. Television shows may assault us, malls may deafen us, Internet ads may track us down everywhere—yet something stops us from spending an afternoon reading a glamour magazine while two attendants administer pedicures to our tired feet. Perhaps our sense of contentment is linked to personal growth.

Sure, I love the big things money can buy, but what really makes me clap my hands with glee are the childish delights of life—those that nurture the best version of me. I just needed to recover the confidence to admit them into my world.

'Look, Natasha, this isn't working for you at all,' my friend Shefali said one day. She had come to meet me at home and then insisted that we walk to a coffee shop—to 'take you out of the house'. Our third child was under a year old and I guess I looked desperate. Shefali had her camera with her and she took a few pictures of me.

'Staying at home is terrible for you,' she said, putting down the camera. 'You've tried it, you keep falling ill, you write strange status updates . . . now just give up this idea.'

'No, no, I have to be here,' I said to her. 'I feel like I am putting broken pieces of myself back together.' My voice cracked a little even as my words themselves sounded broken.

Sure, I was upset a lot, but just because I was no good at being at home didn't mean I didn't want to be there. I had rejected many of the hand-me-down ideas of how to run a family and raise children. I had said no-thank-you to new, lucrative work roles. In the middle of my life, I was starting from scratch. It looked like I was doing nothing. But I was healing.

It wasn't easy for us, as a family. I could see my husband's struggle from a distance. I would say to him in my head: 'You are desperate to live your life despite having little children. How about making choices *because* you have them, rather than making choices *despite* having them?'

Of course, I couldn't see myself with the same clarity.

I knew what my husband and I had in common. We didn't want to repeat the mistakes we thought our parents had made. But what did we want?

It takes years to unlearn toxic behaviours. It takes years of stillness to be less greedy; to avoid being rude to those who cannot answer back; to pause and honour a moment of beauty; to listen; to apologize; and to truly treasure what is precious.

I love being around other people's children. I am goofy and cheerful. It's not so effortless when they are my own. I am lost and distracted. This is a common, familiar experience for many adults. First, we are lost among our own peers and then, we feel that we have lost our children, too.

This brings me to another version of why I quit office and came back home. At a party where we were assigning each other animal personas, my best friend called me a Pomeranian. Here I was acting like a big shot, important person and my friend was telling me that I was still a silly little people-pleaser. I needed re-education. Or I needed new friends.

The kids are never more pleased
with me than when I return from
a day of teaching.

"You are a Ma'am?" asks Naseem.

"Yes, I am."

"Do you ask
your students
to sit properly
in the dining
hall?"

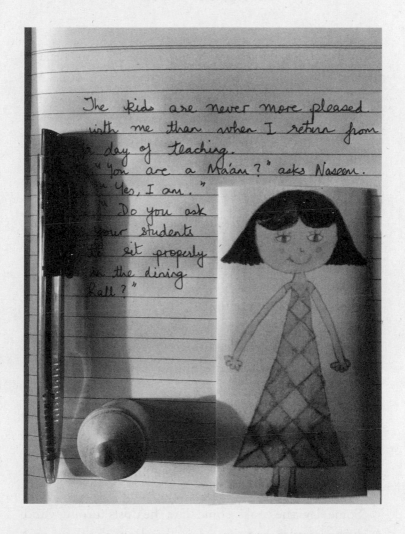

Lessons Learnt from the One Who Helps Me Work

'Why are you making a roti when I asked you to make a parantha? I asked for cheese, not butter, Kanta Mausi.'

I hear the raised voice of our youngest child who is trying to boss over Kanta in the kitchen. It makes me squirm. I am embarrassed. I want to raise my voice even louder and tell her off for speaking so rudely to the woman who has nurtured her.

I hold myself back.

My child is scolding Kanta because she has heard me scold Kanta.

Kanta has been working in our home for over a decade. When we first knew her, she would come for an hour, mop the floors and clean the toilets. She started staying back a bit longer when Ammi was recovering from surgery; she'd give my mother-in-law a leg massage.

There was a time when Kanta was one of three women working in our home. It was a period of abundant chaos. We had many house guests, our children were babies, and both my husband and I spent long hours outside at our workplaces.

Over time, as we got wiser and simplified our lives, Kanta became the only one to work in our home.

Some days she cooks, some days she dusts furniture and folds the laundry, and some days she cleans the floors and bathrooms. Every day she sings to herself.

Apparently, Kanta is not supposed to be a cook. When I first asked her to cook for us, the elders in our family tried to dissuade us by pointing out that her food is not 'hygienic'. At first, that drew a blank—so, we were awkwardly informed that Kanta is a Dalit, a low-caste woman.

Kanta makes the best yellow dal in the world. She is an expert at stuffed paranthas and chutney. Many of our friends stay over just so they can have '*Kanta Mausi ke paranthe*' the next morning.

Kanta and I barely understood each other at first. Her Hindi borrows nouns and verbs heavily from a local dialect, and mine is peppered with English words. Instructions and explanations would fall flat and leave me fuming.

But Kanta has a way of deflating all conflict with a laugh that is disarming. I am fascinated by her dignity and childlike charm. *Emotional literacy is love-centred emotional intelligence*, I read, as I prepare for my next training workshop. The words make sense to me when I consider them in the context of Kanta.

Sometimes Kanta is my mother, bringing me a tall glass of Bournvita-milk, as I slouch at my desk. Often we are friends—two women, happy to be immersed in work, in our own spaces. Some days we are strangers. Sometimes I am a vicious, ungrateful, foul-tempered boss, venting my frustrations on her.

'Look, don't ruin my day, okay,' she will say. 'It's not such a big deal.'

'It is a big deal, Kanta.'

'The only deal is that I need to work because I need the

money to educate my grandchildren,' she will respond, and turn away from me.

Kanta takes care of her parents, in-laws, sons, grandchildren, daughters-in-law, and anyone else who is in need in her neighbourhood. She asks for loans that she passes on to others. She is an excellent negotiator. She demands her annual raise with authority and assertiveness. She reminds me that I had once told her that I would give her half of whatever I earned because she was the one who enabled me to work. It is true; I had said this to her. She deserves it.

Kanta is relaxed and cheerful when my mother visits. They exchange notes on how bratty I am and how sweet my children are. She gets nervous when my in-laws visit. 'Kanta,' I whisper at such times, 'they are not *your* in-laws!' Of course, it suits me that she is hyper-vigilant when my husband's parents are visiting. Everyone gives me credit for the work she does.

Kanta is forever young. She asks for new clothes that are exactly like mine. She is at least two sizes larger than me but she tells me she feels like a lithe sixteen-year-old.

She refuses to learn anything new. I appreciate that. People who are competent and sincere must guard against the tendency to acquire too many skills. Kanta needs all the rest she can get.

What I have learnt most from Kanta is to bide my time; to stay cheerful, even if I am late to work, because I have a full day ahead of me; to be diligent, without becoming edgy; to laugh at my mistakes because life punishes us enough.

Now, Kanta hurries down the steps after putting out the clothes to dry in the upstairs balcony. She balances a large, pink plastic tub like a tambourine and taps her fingers against it to make music.

'I am writing nice things about you, Kanta,' I say to her.

She laughs and sends me a flying kiss—the gesture making her giggle all over again.

A Manifesto for Working Women

In the colony in Ranchi where I spent my early childhood, all women around us worked—not one was unemployed. Sinha Aunty was a farmer. She grew crops in the large backyard of their home. We never returned from her place without bushels of fresh green channa or vegetables. She had three children she nurtured.

My grandmother couldn't see very well any more, yet she sewed and knitted. Mrs Swami was a South Indian food expert and trained many other women, including my mother, in the art of making idlis, dosas and chutneys.

The men—like so many other men—'went to work'. They had designations and received salaries. They got promotions. They went on tours. They were important. We celebrated their achievements on weekends and in special parties. Families depended on them.

It was a very dissonant world for me. I admired my mother, but I wanted to be like my father. I wanted to travel. I wanted credit for my intelligence. I wanted to be a part of a larger world that all men seemed to slip into with ease. I wanted to become somebody—unlike my mother who apparently was a nobody. There were very few women we saw working outside their homes. There were the Irish and Malayali nuns and other teachers in our convent school. There was one female doctor in the city hospital, a gynaecologist. And there were tribal women who worked as maids in our homes.

Sure enough, I grew up and became a 'working woman'—and spent eight of those years as a 'single working woman'. Our parents had saved and struggled and moved jobs and cities to make sure we got an education that would prepare us to become independent adults—so there I was, 'respectfully employed'.

In 2007, I went independent. I became a media trainer and a consultant. I began to write a regular column in a national newspaper. After twenty years of being a working professional, here is what I want to add to the conversation about women at work: Women are always at work. We need to start honouring the work we do every day.

A global culture that calls it 'work' only when it is remunerated needs to be challenged with a new language and framework. The spotlight that shines so brightly on what women are not doing needs to be redirected towards the invisible work they do throughout their lives.

There is a crisis of self-esteem that assails most women. Unacknowledged fatigue and unarticulated responsibilities bog us down. We berate ourselves for not knowing and doing better. We have to change mindsets not only at a social level but also at an individual level.

Here is a quick manifesto for working women, for all women:

Nobody can rescue us. No. Not unless we want to rescue ourselves. Nothing will inspire change in our lives unless we actively seek inspiration and growth.

Change is hard work. It threatens status quo and demands patience. It asks for introspection and learning. It pushes us outside our safety zones. We cannot achieve it in isolation. We need to learn to ask for help.

Ask for help without surrendering your autonomy. Seek answers to questions—no matter how obvious—so you can make informed decisions. Dissect the narratives of others and take what you need to from their stories.

Don't internalize disapproval. Often the people we love the most—the family whose approval matters to us—don't support our efficient, multitasking personas. The men in our lives may feel threatened by our self-sufficiency. Recognize their feelings for what they are. Find ways to deal with the conflict without stepping back. Don't forsake your responsibility towards yourself.

Tune out the noise. Identify what you have internalized while growing up. This reveals itself slowly. It asserts itself, for instance, in your immediate reaction to the news that a friend with a demanding job is getting married. Or is pregnant. Or has quit. Pay attention to the assumptions and judgements that your mind makes in such situations. These are judgements you make about yourself, too. Do I deserve better? Are my ambitions worthwhile? Am I good enough? The answer to all these questions is 'yes'.

Change the internal narrative. We cannot even *begin* to challenge other people's attitudes without first examining our own set of prejudices. If we go on repeating that child-rearing is dirty work, it sure will feel like that. If we deny others the autonomy to make personal choices, we hem ourselves in, too.

Own your time and space. Also give yourself the permission to own your money. Society hasn't handed these privileges to women on a platter. That does not mean that we cannot claim them. We can.

At the same time, we don't have to swing from one set of pre-determined choices to another. We have the right and the power within us to redefine success and to spell out our own priorities and goals at different stages. The narrative that women and mothers must compromise their ambitions and neglect their talents for the greater good of the family is a lie. Don't accept it.

The Wanderer

In a traffic jam, inside our car —

Child 1 : I am 100 percent convinced our
life will be spent stuck in a jam.
Child 2 : Has been spent! I have
spent 5 years in a car and 5 years in
the world. And I am 10.
Child 3 : Mamma, they are not putting my
song on the stereo.

Be Corny, Bold and Silly

I love going away and I love coming back home.

I love leaving home because *vasudhaiva kutumbakam*—the world is my family. Unless I set myself adrift, how can I discover the people I am related to? Besides, I love sitting on sidewalks and somehow that happens a lot when I travel. I walk a great deal, I get tired and sit by a kerb, preferably near a street food vendor. I rest, I eat and I belong.

Talking about looking for people I am related to, I must confess that I avoid my own relatives. I divide the time allocated for real-life relatives like this: 99 per cent for my husband's relatives and 1 per cent for my own. I spend more time with my husband's relatives because they don't know me, they have low expectations and I love to surprise them every once in a while. Sometimes when I relax, I actually earn their approval.

I love my own relatives very much, too. They are very well behaved on Facebook. Sometimes we behave well when we meet also.

Wait, I was talking about travelling, not relatives. They are linked—we travel to get away from relatives and create new ones. We also travel to relate to ourselves.

Last year, when I was packing to go on a shoot to Chhattisgarh, I found myself pumping my fist in the air, while also looking at my list to make sure I wasn't forgetting anything.

'Yes!' I was going away. 'Yay!'

And yes, I had finished organizing our children's school uniforms for the next day or two.

I mentioned this to my colleague at the airport the next morning. I described how physically happy I was. 'Oh, that's sad,' he said. 'You don't like being with your children?' Perhaps he also felt sorry for my husband, my house plants and the street dogs I feed leftover dinner to every other night.

'Oh no, no, I just love to leave home,' I said, dreamily, as we inched forward in the early morning queue at the security barrier. I remember I was wearing a cotton sari with a printed blouse. I love leaving home so much that sometimes I wake up at 4.30 am to bathe and wear a sari to celebrate the occasion.

'Your mother has wings,' I told my children when I was leaving them in their grandparents' home to travel to Bundelkhand to conduct a video training workshop. 'She flies so that you can also fly one day.' The children's schools had shut for summer holidays, and we were all visiting my in-laws in their home. All my daughters were hugging me as I spoke to them.

I often say corny things to my children. I am corny.

I also love coming back home. I keep a special outfit for my return. I enjoy being welcomed back. Maybe it's that phase in life—when the children are just the right age—happy to see one go and just as happy to see me return.

My husband was seeing me off at the Varanasi railway station for that trip to Karwi, Bundelkhand. We had reached early, and were seated on my berth in the train and talking.

He had bought me fresh jamuns sprinkled with rock salt from a vendor at the station. Soon, we were joined by an elderly woman who was being seen off by some men in her family. They made sure she was comfortable and then began to leave. All of them touched her feet deferentially before leaving.

Soon it was time for my husband to leave. Without dropping a clue, he bent down and touched my feet, too. Then we shook hands, trying not to grin too hard. I said to him, 'You can smooch me now to complete the ritual.' He laughed his embarrassed laugh—his mouth making a vain attempt to remain closed while his teeth shone through.

Then he left. Then he came back. 'Why should I go early when the train is not leaving yet?'

He sat down. The next time he began to leave, I said I had to return the favour and bent and touched his feet. Then, I got off the train and stood on the platform with him. Now, we were outside the window of the woman who was going to be my travelling companion. We shook hands all over again, aware that we were being watched. I returned to my seat and began to eat jamuns.

When my phone rang, my companion was more than mildly curious about who I was and where I was coming from. I spoke to my sister-in-law in Urdu. Then, on the next call, I spoke to the journalists who were going to receive me in Karwi and mentioned the camera equipment they had to bring. Then, when my kids called I spoke to them in gibberish. My companion's expression was priceless. What was she to make of me?

I want to talk to the traveller in you—the maverick child and the errant adult who hasn't run free for a while. Be by yourself, meet strangers, fall in love with life for a bit. Be wilful, be strange, do things that aren't expected of you. Be unpredictable and a little disruptive. Even unoriginal, if you wish—like people in the movies and books, all tear-jerkers that you love to hate so much.

Travelling for World Peace

Travelling together as a family is important for world peace—but, really, the main reason for getting our bags packed and into the car was that it was much too cold at home that January.

Just before our impromptu trip, my husband had been spending his working hours looking up six types of portable room heaters available in four markets within a 5 kilometre radius of our home. He had measured the length, breadth and height of our misshapen home and calculated how hot and cold air would interact if a medley of new heaters happened to get installed in strategic positions. All I was doing to help him—from my spot near the dual-rod carbon heater—was point to where the draught came from. The short answer was—everywhere.

Leaving home for a road trip to Madhya Pradesh seemed to be the perfect solution. Schools were shut for another two weeks. We got late leaving home because we had invited a friend to join us at the last minute. By the time he arrived with his bags and we got on to the Expressway—New Delhi to Gwalior—I was already missing Gwalior. The sun had begun to set and the light filtering into our car was glorious and warm.

We got lost in the traffic of Agra for a while. Our friend, Gaurav, almost drove over the shoes of a traffic policeman as we veered towards him to ask for directions. Everyone seemed to know which way Gwalior was, but it took us a while to figure out the twists and turns, and get on to the highway again.

When we finally reached, our children loved the bathroom at the heritage hotel. It was as big as our room. From our windows, we had a view of seventeenth century cenotaphs and old temples, and our balcony opened to a fruit-laden guava orchard with peacocks and scampering puppies. My husband was overawed by the restoration work in the hotel, and could not stop expressing his admiration. He made me take photographs everywhere.

'I don't understand what Papa finds so nice about this place,' nine-year-old Aliza told her elder sister.

'It's nice because it is very old,' Sahar explained.

'I like the tomato and cheese salad,' said Aliza, consoling herself.

'I like the bathtub,' added Naseem, our youngest.

'Why have I not seen this in a film before?' our friend wondered as we drove past imposing Jain statues carved into hills on our way to the Gwalior Fort. Gaurav is a young cinematographer.

Besides our primary desire to escape winter in our ice-box home, we had also chosen to travel the Delhi–Gwalior route because Sahar had been to Gwalior on a school trip. Being a me-too person, I wanted to experience with my firstborn what she had enjoyed with her friends and teachers.

'This is where I bought green chips, Mamma!' Sahar exclaimed as we got off near the fort's main gate. 'There was a man selling cotton candy right here.'

This is what children's memories are made of, I thought

to myself. I was happy to see the corner shop from which my daughter had independently bought her first packet of potato chips. I'm a soppy parent and I am not ashamed to admit it.

We moved towards an ancient well and the fort elevation decorated with rows of yellow ducks. Sahar showed us spots where her friends and she had played pakdampakdai, dog-and-the-bone and a game called knock-knock-chicklets.

As we turned the corner—the entire city of Gwalior suddenly visible—I spotted a woman selling imli and phalse, alongside packets of paan masala. I bought five rupees worth of raw tamarind, sprinkled with salt and loosely wrapped in a newspaper.

'What is your name?' the woman asked our six-year-old daughter.

'Naseem,' she said.

'What is your name?' I asked her.

'Meera,' she replied.

'Wah!' I said, thinking at once of Meerabai, the mystic poet.

'Are you Muslims?' she asked Naseem.

Naseem looked at me for the answer.

'Say yes,' I told her. 'We are Muslims.'

'Naseem is a lovely name,' said the imli-seller, as my daughter tentatively tasted tamarind for the first time.

'Meera is a lovely name, too,' I said.

'You must be Pathans,' she smiled. She liked us.

'Umm, we are Mughals, actually,' I told her. I pronounced Mughals as 'muggles' to feel less like an imposter.

I ran to my husband to report the conversation to him. 'I made your mother proud,' I said. Ammi often liked to remind us that her granddaughters were Mughlanis.

This is my policy in life. Adopt every identity you run into. Be everyone. There are so many selves to embrace.

Aliza was running around with Gaurav's still camera. She took photos of the graffiti on the walls—names on stone, carved by tourists, for others to read. I did not ask her why this was all she wanted to document. While my daughter was chasing graffiti, I was busy admiring the intricate lattice and meenakari work in the Gwalior Fort.

We were distracted by parakeets. A squirrel darted close to a flock of birds to get his share of lunch.

'Where did you see the sound-and-light show?' I asked Sahar.

She couldn't quite remember. 'My friends bought gifts from here.' She pointed to a curio stand.

Afzal purchased some channa-jor-garam and was aghast when I reported that I had never eaten this roadside snack before. 'I have only heard it mentioned in the movies,' I told him, just so we could all see him roll his eyes at my ignorance.

Aliza chose to sit on my lap for long stretches of the road trip. She had an upset stomach, and this position kept her close to me and also allowed her to change the radio channels on the car stereo till she found a song she liked.

'What is your weight, Aliza?' I asked, readjusting her on my lap.

'30 kilos,' she said. 'But I was wearing my jacket and

shoes and sweater when I stood on the weighing machine in my school.' She turned and looked at me for reassurance.

I want to hold on to her child-voice and celebrate these moments of innocence. I want to underline that it is okay to not know the facts. It is important to know feelings and be able to express them before they mutate into skin allergies and asthma attacks and migraines. I want my daughters to always have the confidence to ask for help and receive it when they need it.

We came back home a few days later. I sat next to my beloved heater all night to type this. I needed some water, but the kitchen was cold and I was lazy. Okay, okay, I'll drink some water now. Thank you for your company.

Naseen's memory of
the trek —
"Every time we heard
bells, we would stand
by the side of the
mountain in a line,
waiting for the mules
to pass. As if the
mules were the Queen
and we were common
people waiting to let it
pass."
She laughs.

At Home in the Entire World

The man I bought groundnuts from in Mandawa, had light eyes just like my husband. I stared at his face. Thick, hard lines. He did not respond to my small talk in Hindi. He spoke Shekhawati. The groundnuts were very good. I must have been hungry.

We did not bathe every day. We admired clean bathrooms. And washrooms. The sand, shrubs and horizon—they were there when we chose to take a break on the highway instead of waiting for a toilet. I took photos of the children and me every time we caught a reflection of ourselves in a mirror.

The middle child cried for home. She said she would never go on a holiday again. We slowed down. Later, she said she loved Jaisalmer. She wished it were closer to her home. On the last day, everyone was sad it was the last day.

We ate a lot. Sometimes we ate very late. It is not a good idea to stay hungry for long. The parents had debates about this. The mother learnt to spend money on food rather than shopping.

The children bought pens studded with tiny mirrors. The mother thought they were common trinkets. The children were in awe of their new-found treasure. They bought notebooks with covers made from fabric from Banarasi silk saris. The youngest got a smaller notebook to draw in. She carried her crayons and colouring books everywhere. Her lilac bag had once been her mother's favourite. It pleased her mother to think about her solo adventures with the same bag strapped across her chest.

They read slogans on the backs of trucks. They counted camels. And donkeys. A white horse. Deer and nilgai. A rabbit dashed across the road. A pair of peacocks preened on a roof as they drove through Fatehpur.

We must come back here again.

The children asked a lot of questions. 'I love it when you ask me questions,' said the mother. She turned around from the front seat of the car and answered. The father drove like he was a seatbelt-wearing superhero. He never seemed to get tired or sleepy.

Rohit, a friend of the parents and children—and a fellow companion on this journey—was a Gulzar fan. Every song he played in the car inspired a storytelling session. The children listened with worried faces. Sometimes, they hated what happened in the story and quickly searched for a distraction.

Songs from Gulzar's film *Lekin* played in the car as they drove through the desert in Rajasthan. The mother said she was looking for the ghost of the desert. The father said he was looking for Dimple Kapadia. The children slept a lot in the car. They narrated their dreams when they woke up. More stories.

'Where are you from?' everyone asked us.

'We are from Delhi,' we said.

'Are you from Delhi proper?'

Sometimes we said yes. Sometimes we named other places.

'The Aam Aadmi Party has spoilt the mood,' said one man near Jaisalmer Fort. 'Prices have soared. This country needs Narendra Modi.'

We nodded with him.

'Delhi!' said a young man in a shop. 'The Aam Aadmi Party has changed the game there. We are all *aam aadmi*. This is good for us.'

We nodded with more enthusiasm.

The children sat down on whatever they could find in the shop. The men talked about the country. The mother bought more gifts from the shop than she had intended to.

'I want lip balm for myself,' said one of the children. She got a green lip balm stick with a key chain attached to it. Later the family bought small locks with tiny keys from Mandawa. The kids discussed how they would lock their secret diaries and hide the keys. The parents looked at each other, silently marking this new stage in their lives.

Everyone loved buffet breakfasts. We got tired of tandoori rotis. We discovered *bajre ki roti*. We ate lots of butter. We saw baby camels and royal cenotaphs. We were the last people in the evening to enter the Jain temple in the heart of Bikaner.

'I have just changed out of my Pandit's clothes,' said the priest apologetically. He was wearing a shirt and trousers now.

'We are sorry we are late,' we replied.

Two of the children had ice cream cones in their hands. We wondered if they should enter the temple.

'Never mind,' he said, glancing in their direction. 'Children are excused.'

The priest took Rohit's smartphone, flipped the camera to self-portrait mode, and placed it on the floor in the centre of the temple. He showed us how to take the best photos of the murals on the ceiling. He took photos of us, for us. We noted down the names of the galis, chowks, bhujia shops and havelis he told us about. He knew more about Bikaner than the Internet does. I should have taken a photo of the Jain priest. He had big hair and a bigger smile.

A dramatic ochre sky framed silent windmills as the sun set in the desert. In the streets, we looked at people and people looked at us. It was a fair exchange. Rajasthan hosted us with warmth and care.

Our home looked beautiful as I switched off the burglar alarm and opened the door. When you find yourself at home in the entire world, you can also find the entire world in your own home.

'Take breaks. Go for lots of holidays,' a friend had once advised me very seriously. 'Come back home and live your own lives, but go on as many holidays together as you can.'

This must be what she was talking about.

A Household in a Car and the Stars Above

We started with an invocation.

'As we begin this journey, those of us who know how to, should pray,' I said.

'Prayer?' asked six-year-old Naseem. 'Why should we do that?'

'We pray to god to stay with us and keep us safe as we travel together.'

To my surprise, Sahar and Aliza, our older daughters, turned towards each other and began to mutter a chant they had learnt from their Arabic teacher.

I was impressed. If and when I pray, I do so in English.

Then, my daughters started giggling.

'What happened?' I asked.

'We were saying the prayer that is supposed to be said after eating a meal,' they replied.

Ashok, our driver, switched on the car radio. '*Teri hai zameen, tera aasman, tu bada meherbaan, tu bakshish kar . . .*' came the song from the 1980s Hindi film *The Burning Train*.

The earth belongs to you, the sky belongs to you, you are ever generous . . .

Naseem has learnt this song in school and began to sing along. Just like that, she got in her own prayer.

This is going to seem almost implausible when I write about it, I thought to myself.

It had been an impromptu decision to drive all the way from our home in New Delhi to our village in the farthest corner of eastern Uttar Pradesh. We had train tickets—but we discovered at the last minute that they had not been confirmed. Our children and I had planned to join my husband, who was already in the village. I was inclined to call off the journey. But my daughters were firm—they wanted to see their dad.

'Come by road,' my husband urged over telephone. I let the family lead me. It was only 900 kilometres, after all. It was early evening by the time we began the drive from our home.

As we got on to the Yamuna Expressway, I took Aliza's arm and traced a map on it. Delhi–Agra–Kanpur–Allahabad–Varanasi–Ghazipur. And then a small dot for the village where my in-laws lived and where my husband had work projects.

We approached Firozabad. The name evoked conflicting images—of some of the most exquisite glassware in India; of raids to rescue kids working as cheap labour near blazing furnaces. I realized I had never been to this small town before. We slowed down at a crossing. Everywhere I looked, men were transporting freshly-made glass bangles by bicycles and handcarts. The bangles glinted, illuminated by headlights.

We played memory games in the car. The youngest was best able to remember a string of unrelated, random words. She won each time.

'Don't stop at Etawah for dinner, carry on to Kanpur,' a friend texted me. 'Etawah is not safe at night.' She knew the route we were taking.

A flood of memories. One of my most dramatic news shoots has been in Mainpuri and Etawah. My colleague Barkha and I had been investigating a story on illegal country-made guns. It was election season. As broadcast journalists, we depended on insiders and locals to lead us deep into the heart of the narrative we needed on videotape.

In Mainpuri, we had met a man at a gun shop in the main market and told him that we were exploring a story on country-made pistols and ammunition. He had peculiar scars on his face and couldn't speak very clearly. He had been shot through his cheek in a local gang war and had spent months in a Singapore hospital getting his face surgically reconstructed. His tongue had been injured, too.

I described this adventure to my daughters as we drove past Mainpuri in the darkness.

'Did he have two circles on his cheeks?' Sahar asked me, trying to imagine a man who had had a bullet slice through his face. I smiled at her and looked away. I remembered the terror and awe I had felt that night as we let him lead us to a factory where unlicensed guns were being manufactured.

We got out of the car at a petrol station to stretch our legs. The children began to dance. One of them was singing a song from *Frozen* and the other two were mimicking Gloria, the hippopotamus from *Madagascar*.

I stopped myself from stopping them. Let them own their world, I thought. Let them dance in Etawah in the middle of the night.

Then, I told myself: Forget to take your fears with you sometimes, just like you forget to pick up your phone charger or boarding pass before you leave home.

'When will our hotel come?' asked Naseem. She wanted to sleep in a bed now.

'In two hours,' I said.

'Up to what do I have to count for two hours to be over?'

'Forty thousand,' I said randomly.

She began to count. I felt sheepish. She reached 1,040, then turned to me.

'I have counted so much. Where is the hotel?'

She'd soon sleep in my arms. I held hands with my firstborn. We claimed our intimacy whenever we got a chance.

At 3 am, we admired a crescent of a moon in the sky as we decided not to stop in Kanpur for the night. The sky was dark, and then, one by one, the children began to spot the stars. Ashok, our driver, had never travelled out of Delhi before and this trip was equally exciting for him.

As Ashok continued to drive through the night, all of us drifted into sleep, and woke up in an untidy Varanasi at dawn. We heard the Gayatri Mantra on a loudspeaker. I sang along, trying to match the vocalist's scale. This was the only prayer I had known as a child, and it became a part of our journey, too.

When we stopped for tea, the children had Taka-Tak, Mad Angles, Kurkure and Lay's for breakfast. They discovered free toys in the plastic bags. If their father had been with us, he would have led them towards puri sabzi and samosa. We chose to stop at Sidhauna for rasgulla and gulab jamun. Make a note of this place, I told my daughters grandly, this is a world-famous stopover in eastern Uttar Pradesh. Ignore the flies.

I watched my children from a distance, leaning on a dusty car on a highway, chatting with each other, sharing their snacks, and being friendly with a stray dog. This picture is exactly where I wanted to reach when I started out on this journey years ago. I didn't have a map, but I did have a plan.

I feel most at home with my family when we are away from our house—when we are between homes. Everyone is free and we are all together. This is the definition of family for me.

Returning to a Place of the Past

For more than twenty years after I left that city, I refused to belong to the new one I had moved to. Calcutta was the home of my childhood. It had captured my imagination and Delhi did nothing to move me.

I was seven years old when I first arrived in Calcutta. I had boarded a flight from Ranchi, without my family, in the company of my father's colleague, to take a school entrance exam in the city. My father was already there—he picked me up at the airport and took me to Ashok Hall School. Perhaps it was my first grown-up moment—arriving in a new city by aeroplane and being received by my father.

After almost three decades, I went back to the city for work. The taxi I took at the airport was an Ambassador car—so old that I wondered if it had been around since I had last been here. Maybe I have sat in this car before, I thought, as it took me through the streets at midnight.

We passed Gariahat. I could hear the noise and commotion from my childhood, my parents haggling with shopkeepers, their three small children in tow. I remembered the humidity on our skin.

I learnt to lie in Calcutta. When I wanted new colour pencils, but was afraid I wouldn't get them, I lied that it was compulsory to take them to school. I remember feeling guilty when my parents bought me a new set of a dozen pencils. I started crying in this market, somewhere in Gariahat.

Bhai, my older brother, played football in this city. He learnt to play the sitar in his school orchestra. It was quite an achievement—buying an elegant sitar from someone's home and carrying it in a public bus all the way to our home.

My younger brother Manu and I played in the street outside our home in New Alipore. There was an open drain on one side. A milkman's family lived in one of the empty plots. Manu used to play with the milkman's son. For them playing meant fighting. They got entangled in a Bengali man's legs one day, as they were wrestling with each other. The man's white dhoti came undone. He was so angry, he dropped his umbrella and began to smack both the six-year-olds. Manu was fine soon enough, but I cried hysterically for a long time afterwards.

'Did he beat you also?' my friends asked me.

'No, he beat my brother,' I said between sobs.

'Then why are you crying?' they asked.

'He beat my brother,' I kept repeating.

Now I was back as a grown-up woman. The next morning, I deliberately chose to ride on a cycle-rickshaw. I made a video of the city's streets, recording familiar sights as I took them in. There were white kittens. Fresh yellow flowers on a creeper across an old iron gate. A Jyoti Basu poster on a wall—which almost bridged the thirty years between my visits to this city.

The first time a school bus had brought me home from school, the bus conductor had to wake me up at my stop. I remember his face. I couldn't tell where I was. My mother had gone to pick up my brothers from another bus stop. The conductor got the school bus parked and took me around the neighbourhood to help find my home. It must have been cute—a groggy seven-year-old trying to find her new home in an unfamiliar street.

One day, Bhai returned from school with a fractured arm. I was mesmerized. I tried to get a fractured arm, too. I kept pushing my elbow out of the school bus window till it grazed against a parked truck. I didn't know how to stop the bleeding—and I didn't want a fracture any more after that.

My mother let me go for a haircut to the barber at the end of the street all by myself. I carried a *Richie Rich* comic in my hand and showed him Gloria's long, blonde tresses.

'I want a haircut like this,' I said.

I had short hair. It was called a 'boy-cut' back then. The barber gave me a haircut. I was so disappointed I could have cried. I came home and read *Asterix* comics to console myself.

We were in Calcutta when the news arrived that my mother's mother had died. She left for Delhi with my younger brother immediately. I was diagnosed with chicken pox while she was away. Our neighbours from downstairs supported my father as he struggled to send Bhai to school, tend to me at home, and somehow manage his office work as well.

While Mummy was away, Papa cooked for us. He made aloo gobi in the pressure cooker one evening. It was watery and bland. Papa was gentle and soft-spoken with us when Mummy was not at home. 'Don't I make pretty good rotis?' he said, trying to cheer us up.

I went to our Bengali neighbours' home and returned with alta on my feet one day. Papa hated it. I washed it off too soon, heartbroken. I'll give it a chance another day, a boundary of red around the soles of my feet. Alta reminds me of goddesses.

We used to go pandal-hopping on our scooter during Durga Puja.

Midway through our Calcutta years, we bought a TV set. We were late adopters. On cricket match days and Sunday film evenings, children would crowd outside the windows of homes that had a TV set to catch a glimpse of the wonders it held. Bhai spent hours tuning the television so it would pick up the signal from Dhaka. They showed *Star Trek* in Bangladesh in the late 1970s.

My mother was preparing to bake a cake when the telegram came with the news that my father's mother had died in Jalandhar. She sat down, holding her face in her hands, and sobbed. 'My mother loves my grandmother,' I remember thinking.

Childhood is a box of things—the string that we wound around our wooden top; my doll's broken arm; glass marbles; the packets of Wrigley's and Big Red that Mum kept in her Godrej almirah so they'd last for years; Papa cleaning his scooter on Sunday mornings; the handwritten letters from our family in Delhi, Punjab and abroad.

I went back to that Calcutta and had to keep reminding myself to spell it as Kolkata. Okay, okay, I will call you

Kolkata, I surrendered, feeling annoyed that my childhood
friend had taken on a new name.

'If you leave me anywhere, I'll find my way to my old
home in New Alipore,' I remember telling my Delhi friends.
I know the route to my childhood home like the back of
my hand.

The Feminist

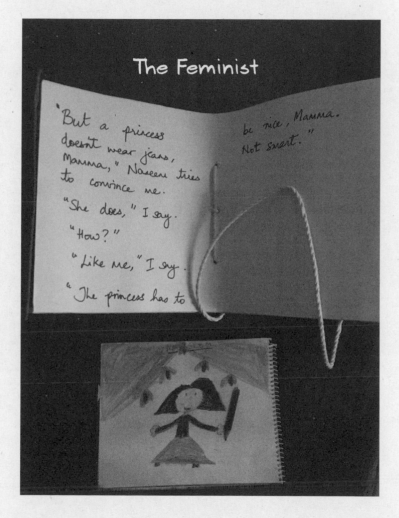

"But a princess doesn't wear jeans, Mamma," Naseem tries to convince me.

"She does," I say.

"How?"

"Like me," I say.

"The princess has to be nice, Mamma. Not smart."

The Right to Choose How She Is Represented

Our middle child sat angrily with her Hindi homework. She had to write an essay on what she wanted to be when she grew up.

'That's an easy one,' I said to her. 'What do you want to be?'

'I don't know, Mamma,' she replied.

'That's fine. You can write that you are interested in a lot of things but have not made up your mind.'

'I want to be a criminal,' she said with much emphasis.

'Like Robin Hood?' I asked, hopefully.

'No. I want to be a real criminal. I will kill people.'

I suspect that if Aliza had been a nine-year-old son, I would have been very worried indeed. But Aliza is a very quiet and gentle child, and the novelty of her outpouring amused me.

'I want to be a criminal because the good people are all bad people and the bad people are good people,' she elaborated.

I think I know what she means. She is trying to make sense of the same world that we have all become exhausted outraging against. We switch on the radio in the car and we switch it off in disgust. Sometimes it is because of an RJ offering us entertainment by calling up unsuspecting people and humiliating them on air. Sometimes it is because of the lyrics of a new song where a man tells a woman that he's the son of a Jat and he just doesn't take no for an answer.

Recently, I found a document with a list of ideas for future essays. Point Number 4 read: 'It is safer to let one's daughters play with Barbie dolls than it is to allow unrestricted access to mainstream newspapers today. One day, I want to offer myself for public slaughter by making this argument. One day, not today.'

I never did write an essay on the subject—not even when an Indian newspaper stooped really low when confronted by one of India's most popular Hindi film actors, Deepika Padukone.

Padukone had called out the newspaper's 'regressive tactics' and had written: '[. . .] digging out an old article and headlining it "OMG: Deepika's Cleavage Show!" to attract readers is using the power of influence to proliferate recessive thought.' The newspaper in question responded by drawing a red circle around her cleavage in another photograph, and splashing more pictures of her in its supplement. Headlines sought to diminish her argument by calling her a hypocrite for insisting that she had a right to choose how she wished to be represented.

At about the same time, another actor, Emma Watson, delivered a speech on feminism and gender at the United Nations headquarters. She said:

> I think it is right that I should be able to make decisions about my own body. I think it is right that women be involved on my behalf in the policies and decision-making of my country. I think it is right that socially I am afforded the same respect as men.

For years, in our own separate, isolated ways, my husband and I used to worry about the world in which our children were growing up. These days, we have begun to talk about it without the conversation deteriorating into a confused, emotional argument between ourselves.

We watched the video of Watson delivering her speech at the UN. She walked up to the podium and took her place with poise before beginning to address a room full of accomplished people.

Naseem, then six years old, used to often take a day off from school to catch up with her personal life.

'Looks like Hermione to me,' she said.

'It is her,' I replied.

Watson's voice rang through:

These rights, I consider to be human rights [. . .] my parents didn't love me less because I was born a daughter. My school did not limit me because I was a girl. My mentors didn't assume that I would go less far because I might give birth to a child one day.

One part of me watched to see if she would refer to her written notes. She didn't.

I've seen young men suffering from mental illness unable to ask for help for fear it would make them look less 'macho'—in fact in the UK suicide is the biggest killer of men between 20–49 years of age, eclipsing road accidents, cancer and coronary heart disease. I've seen men made fragile and insecure by a distorted sense of what constitutes male success. Men don't have the benefits of equality either.

Did Watson say anything that has not been said before? Does Padukone ask for something out of the ordinary when she seeks basic respect? Yet, these words have not been heard enough. They haven't been validated sufficiently.

'You might be thinking, who is this *Harry Potter* girl?' Watson laughed towards the end of her speech. 'And what is she doing speaking at the UN?'

'It is Hermione!' said Naseem excitedly. 'She said *Harry Potter*! I have to tell Sahar and Aliza when they return home that you two were watching Hermione alone!'

Naseem's sisters came home and listened to the speech, too. Watson was using very big words so Sahar switched on the subtitles.

'What do you like about Hermione?' I asked them later.

'She always thinks things through. She makes plans and is very organized,' said Sahar.

'Hmm,' I responded.

'She is very hard-working but she has her own sense of fun,' added Aliza.

'Plus she is very, very wise.'

In Praise of the *Dehati Aurat*

I stayed in Sonti and Inder Singh's home for four months that summer. My backpack hung from a nail on a wooden pillar in their home, my two books and diary were kept on a ledge. The toddler in their house would prop himself up on my knees and keep me company. He was always hungry and so was I.

1992 had been declared a year of drought in Jhabua district in Madhya Pradesh. The mango trees yielded no fruit that season, the jamun tree dropped wrinkled berries on the dry earth below. With the rains having failed, small farmers could barely harvest enough jowar and bajra to feed their families. They had little money to buy food, even from the ration shops in the tehsil.

The village I was in was Khodamba. It was a four-hour walk, across brown, bare hills, from the nearest bus stop. That bus stop was a six-hour dusty road journey from Alirajpur, the tehsil headquarter. I was teaching the Bhil children and teenagers of Khodamba to read and write Hindi and do basic maths. There was no school in their village. For the most part, they laughed at me. Sometimes, they felt sorry and tried to indulge me.

I received no letters from home while I was there. I collected dried leaves and stuck the first lice retrieved from my hair in my diary. I made notes about cows that ate human faeces—waiting patiently for us to finish our business and leave, so as to get some grain in their diet.

Sonti, my hostess, wondered about the place that I had come from. She could see that I read and wrote a lot, but couldn't bring back a pot of water from the well for my own bath. I was a grown woman, but I seemed helpless like a child. Hungry, dirty, useless and miserable.

Sonti asked me if, where I came from, I had land to grow food. No, I didn't. She asked me if I had cows and hens. No, I didn't. She tried to make sense of the situation. Had I come to her village because there was nothing for me back home? Was I desperately poor?

I had just completed a graduate course in psychology from Delhi University. I wanted to travel, teach and engage meaningfully with the world around me. I was hungry for experience and adventure, and longed to discover my own potential.

Twice a day, Sonti cooked one, large, thick roti for each family member and me. There was some salt, a very watery lentil soup—and that's it. She went to the forest to get firewood, she went to her fields to prepare them for sowing corn when the rains would come, and she walked far to bring back drinking water.

Sonti sang and danced all night when there was a marriage in the village. She went away to join a couple for three days, in mourning, when their infant child died on the way to the hospital.

One day, she served me a bowl of meat with my *makki ki roti*. A group gathered to watch me eat.

'What is this?' I asked.

Someone described a small animal like a rabbit, another stretched his arms wide to show a larger creature.

'Is it a cow?' I wondered.

'No, no!' they protested.

'Is it hairy? Does it have horns? Is it a fox? A goat?'

They giggled and said confusing things but made sure I ate my share of nourishment that day.

In the remote village, under the stars, I would dream of tomatoes and cucumbers in vivid colours. Some evenings, when my stomach was full, I would watch the sun setting behind undulating hillocks and smoke rising from kitchens in the foreground. It felt like a perfect moment in time. On other afternoons, I would go behind a mango tree, sit on my haunches, hug myself, and cry till I felt lighter.

I made notes on how well I would take care of my students when they came to Delhi. I imagined trying to cross a road near India Gate with the teenagers, just like they had led me through their forests or had waited for me to catch my breath in the hills.

I imagined my host family in my city home. No village woman like Sonti, no 'dehati aurat' had ever sat on the sofa in our living room. I shuddered at the thought that once uprooted from her village in this forest, Sonti might find herself approaching closed car doors at traffic lights in Delhi, trying to sell roses, or plastic Santa Claus masks. Her hungry child would be balanced on her hip. Someone like me would turn her face away from this beggar and change the music on the car stereo, in an attempt to distract herself.

We, in Delhi, have heard the phrase 'dehati aurat' being used freely as an abusive epithet. A senior journalist from Pakistan reported (and later retracted the comment) that

Prime Minister Nawaz Sharif had accused Prime Minister Manmohan Singh of behaving like a 'dehati aurat'—or a petty village woman—who ran to tattle to President Obama instead of solving regional problems independently. Narendra Modi, the then chief minister of Gujarat, referring to this remark, proclaimed that the Indian prime minister had been humiliated and his authority demeaned.

People reveal themselves and their deep-rooted biases all the time. Keen to damage the public image of perceived rivals, they try shaming them by calling them women—*rustic women*.

Both my grandmothers were 'dehati aurats'. They were migrants who crossed borders and rebuilt their homes many times over. They knew how to milk cows and spin thread on a spinning wheel. They woke up before dawn to start their day. They were creative and resourceful. They were planners and troubleshooters. They helped their husbands, sons and daughters seek their destinies. They were generous, like Sonti, the tribal woman from Jhabua.

Sonti's humanity kept me alive even when there was barely enough food for her own children. Her eighteen-month-old son would crawl up to me and hold my breast in the hope of nourishment. In this denuded world, she managed to make space for me and give me a home.

As I acknowledge this 'dehati aurat', I learn to connect with the history that has created me; the blood and sweat that has shaped my soul; the gritty spirit that fights to keep a family alive. I learn patience and I feel gratitude—I wait for a time when our leaders learn to imbibe the power and wisdom of the ordinary village woman.

Aliza is opening her birthday presents,
gift wrapped in paper with Princess and
the Pauper photos.
"I hope it's not a Barbie, I hope it's
not a Barbie," She chants as she cuts
the tape. "I don't want any more Barbies!"
Gift opened.
It is not a Barbie.
You should see her face.

The Stuff of Their Nightmares

She wakes up in the middle of the night.

'There are bad men outside the house. One has dirty teeth. They tried to take me away . . .'

Bleary-eyed, I hold her tight. 'It's a bad dream, sweetheart. No one will hurt you,' I say.

She wants the lights switched on. I switch them on. I keep her in my clasp, patting her, humming soothing sounds. She won't close her eyes for a while. She's four years old.

Where do these fears come from?

On 16 December 2012, a brutal crime committed in South Delhi stunned everyone. A young woman who had boarded a bus with her friend in the evening, had been gang raped by the men on the bus. She, along with her friend, had been beaten with iron rods. Their clothes had been ripped off and they were thrown off the bus on to a road. The woman—nicknamed 'Nirbhaya' or 'Fearless' by the media—struggled to survive the assault in a hospital in New Delhi. Doctors removed her battered intestines after an infection set in. Like everyone else, my husband and I were following the news—the horror of the crime, the extent of her injuries, her battle to live.

I try to shield our children from an overdose of news and mass media consumption. Yet, standing behind my shoulder, our daughter read what was on my computer screen. Something stopped me from closing the open tab. I held my breath. Any moment now, she was going to ask me what rape meant. *What is this word, Mamma? Gang rape?*

She didn't ask.

When the protests started in Delhi, when people began to walk miles to India Gate to demand justice, I let the news come pouring into our home. Police lathi-charged and tear-gassed students. I cried tears of rage. I showed pictures to the children.

'If you hadn't been so young, I would have been there,' I said to them. 'If you had been older, you would have been there.'

I told them about friends who were organizing and participating in the protests. We met them and listened to their experiences. We hugged them.

A few days later, I woke up unusually early. The headline brought the news I dreaded—'Delhi gang-rape victim dies in a Singapore hospital.' It was not unexpected. She had been transferred there as a last resort to save her life. The news that angered me was the next headline: 'Metro stations leading to India Gate sealed.'

The state government had turned against the citizens. Instead of addressing their concerns of security and justice, police had been deployed to stop people from protesting and expressing themselves.

On New Year's Eve, people got together at the bus stop where the young woman and her friend had boarded the bus. *Call her by her real name*, her parents had said to journalists. *We don't want her death to be in vain.* Her name was Jyoti Singh. There was protest music, there were plays and performances—to inspire us to never forget, to fight for change.

'Mamma, you remember we had seen a film where a girl said, "I was bullied, so I bullied. The cycle must stop"?' asked my daughter at dinner.

'Yes,' I said.

'What does bully mean?'

'It means to be rude, to insult and manipulate someone. Some grown-ups are very mean to children. Sometimes parents humiliate their own children.'

We carried on talking. My children shared stories. A bully is someone who takes advantage of your goodness, they decided. Who squashes your innocence and breaks your trust.

In my life, I have done exactly what Jyoti was doing that evening, many times over. As a university student in Delhi, it was my experience that late evening buses were safer than overcrowded ones during the day. After dark, public transport buses had lights on inside and there was usually enough room to ensure that one wasn't groped and mauled.

One evening, I, too, had boarded the wrong bus outside my college. As soon as the bus moved into traffic, and I made eye contact with the bus conductor at the other end, I realized that apart from the male staff, there was no one else on board. The bus didn't seem to be on its regular route. There was no reason for the driver to have stopped and picked me up. As it slowed near the first traffic light, I jumped out of the open door. I was a twenty-two-year-old post-grad student, leaving campus after a late project, to join my family for a late night film show. I remember the movie we were watching that day. I remember, too, the look in the eyes of the men on the bus; how I instinctively knew I had walked into a trap; how I jumped off to save my life. I held my brother's hand and went to sleep in the movie theatre. I was safe now.

I cannot write about this. Yet, how can I not write about this?

I used to think that becoming a parent had made me weak. I had lost my stomach for violence. I realize now that this is my superpower. I see the insanity and full-blown horror of violence with a kind of clarity I cannot ignore.

Children can smell our fear as though it were cheap new paint. They smell apathy, too. And that's the stuff of their nightmares.

We have to make every effort to show them our commitment; carry on the conversation; be the world that they deserve.

Feminism Is My Best Friend

When I first came upon the word in my late teens, I picked it up and kept it with me. It seemed to explain a lot about me to me. Aha, I thought, so all these aspirations, this energy, the frustration and dissonance I feel in my heart is 'feminism'.

Feminism seemed like another term for common sense. It became my best friend. It bailed me out when everyone else warned me that I would drown if I went in too deep.

My feminism makes me restless. It breaks the boundaries around me. It urges me to walk into new spaces like a free child, spontaneous and trusting. It helps me assume my place in the world—as if I am meant to be here.

To be fair, my feminism is a bit of a dolt. It asks questions that seem to make people awkward. It doesn't quite care about *log kya kahenge*, what others will say. My feminism reminds me that I don't have to prove anything to anyone. It reassures me and calms down the people-pleaser in me.

My feminism is loyal. It has stuck around with me even when I've hit rock bottom. It whispers in my ear: 'You are important. You are important. There is a purpose to your life. You will rise again.'

My grandmother, my father's mother, was a powerful woman with only one working lung. She had survived tuberculosis in her youth and went on to do everything that her doctors warned her against. She was admitted to a sanitarium when her third child was just a few months old. She recovered and returned to raise her three sons. I remember watching her blow laboured breaths into a pipe to stoke an open fire in a closed kitchen, even as she went blue in the face.

We were visiting my grandparents' home in Malerkotla, Punjab. It was early in the evening and Dadi asked my elder brother to accompany her to the vegetable market.

'Why is it always him?' my six-year-old self demanded. 'I want to go with you, Dadi.' I was an early equal opportunity activist.

Dadi indulged me and took me along, leaving my brother behind. In a crowded, narrow lane, as she bought bhindi and radish and spinach, her wicker basket became very heavy. On any other day, she'd have instructed her grandson to lift that weight for her. Now, she ran out of breath and sat by a windowsill. I saw that she was old, ill and frail. How were we going to get home? I felt helpless and ashamed because I did not know how to help her.

That day, my feminism taught me to become strong. It taught me to recognize my vulnerabilities. I learnt to upskill, work hard and become competent. I learnt to ask for help.

My feminism lets me choose my battles. It lets me choose my loves. It is enormously patient. It has a vision and goals. *Build, create, soar and wave at everyone from faraway*, it guides me.

'You want to be a diva,' I tease my feminism.

'Don't you?' It presents a dare.

My feminism owes deep apologies to many people I have ridden roughshod over. When I was younger and oversensitive and judgemental, my feminism hurt people. I took sides too quickly, and stuck labels on others. I made mistakes. I learnt to say sorry.

My feminism estranged me from my mother. My feminism took me back to her. I am reminded of every woman whose life has helped create me. I feel gratitude for their existence. I draw from their power. I mourn their unmourned sorrows. Their untold stories knock at my heart and ask to be told.

My feminism has grown. It is maternal. It kicks ass. It protects. It allows me to love even when I feel hate. It is awfully giggly. It is decisive. It looks for role models. It seeks to become one.

My feminism offers me the wisdom to give up on love when that love begins to diminish me. It has taught me to recognize abuse.

Feminism helps me reinvent myself. In fact, it insists on it. It brings me back to myself. It gives me permission to be unique. It makes me fall in love rather quickly, accepting differences and celebrating commonalities. I've come to listen to my intuitive self.

Feminism gives me a language that leads me out of the darkness, words aglow like fireflies leading the way.

You can refer to feminism any way you like, but everyone needs a friend like this.

One of my ardently feminist friends insists she isn't a feminist at all. Every story she writes, every song she sings, every decision she makes liberates her soul further—and yet, she dismisses the word. Another friend is a famous feminist.

She's a powerful role model in public spaces but she isn't fair at all in her personal space.

My feminism teaches me to look beyond facades. It likes to understand things for what they are. It calls out injustice.

One evening, when I was a college student, my grandfather saw me standing at the gate of our colony talking to a young man I knew. He called me to his room later.

'I saw you in the dark alone with a boy,' he said.

'We were talking, Dadaji,' I replied. 'He is my senior in my university.'

'Natasha, *tumhe darr nahin lagta?*' he asked. 'Aren't you afraid?'

'I didn't do anything wrong, Dadaji,' I said.

Later, he called my father and me to his room.

'Your daughter says she is not afraid of anything,' he told my father. There was reproach in his tone. My father looked at me. We knew what my grandfather meant and neither of us agreed with him.

It is taken for granted that a woman should feel shame; she should be afraid to express and assert herself. She is meant to cower when confronted. My feminism makes me fearless. It gives me a moral compass when the adults and peers in my life don't stand by me. It keeps me on the side of justice and fairness.

My feminism is powerful and happy. It leaves its light on everything I touch.

The Friend

Naseem walks fast, mumbling — "This cannot happen. I never want to see your face again..."
She stomps to the next room.
Sohar tells me helpfully, "She's having a break-up. It's part of her game."

What Friends Are For

Some of my friends are dead now.

Tom Dark used to interpret my dreams for me. I miss him when I wake up from an anxious dream and I wish I had his perspective on why my subconscious tortures me in my sleep. Tom seemed to have the third eye and he did not hesitate to share what he could see.

Tom and I knew each other online. Our words connected, the photos were familiar, and we recognized each other's loves and losses.

So many of us spend our lives missing something without being able to put our finger on it. Sometimes it is right there, near us, waiting to be picked up—but we don't know its potential. We have been taught to be wary of the unfamiliar—including strangers.

Yet, strangers become friends—for many of us the most important, nurturing, soul-saving relationships in our lives are our friendships.

A few years ago, when our youngest child turned four, we went on our first road trip as a family of five. As we checked into the mountain resort at Sonapani in Kumaon, I heard Preeti and her friends way before I saw them. I put on my glasses to get a better look at the group of brightly dressed women who were laughing and joking as they soaked in the autumn sun. My first thought was: 'They must be single women. They don't have children yet.'

I was wrong. And I was shocked at myself. Is this how

bored I was? When was the last time I had guffawed loudly among friends? I realized I was in a bit of trouble. All work and no play was making me an awfully dreary person.

Parents have friends. So do grandparents. Let's just admit it, though. Families don't trust friends. We are suspicious of each other's friendships. Is it necessary to spend time with outsiders? How can we get along with someone so different from us—so much older or younger? How can we even conceive of being intimate with a person we have just met? Or never met? Do we have the courage to nurture a friendship with our child? Or spouse?

Get on with the real stuff.

When I was in my twenties, many of my closest friends were far older than me. Now that I am older, I love the fact that many of my friends are so much younger. I boss them around. I don't always take their calls and I respond to their messages fairly late. I learn so much from them.

Make friends. Your life depends on it. Let your lovers and beloveds have their friends. Your sanity depends on it. Friends are the free gifts you get from the universe. Claim them.

Friends are the ones who smell of coffee. They let you sit on the kerb with them. They are the ones whose landline numbers you still remember. They are the first home you had cycled to. They are the email you haven't acknowledged but still remember as the message you long to respond to. They are cricket buddies and bus stop confidantes. Mentors or protégés. They are of all sorts—those whose words open the soul; who vanish for years; who demand their pound of flesh; who are jealous and needy. Sometimes, they are siblings.

You know a relationship has worked when you can call someone a friend.

Some of my friends are awfully whiny. Some are super-rich but feel poor. I have crabby friends. A couple of them fight with me for not fighting with them. They need an argument to feel loved.

With some of my friends, our relationship is too formal or awkward for us to admit that we are actually friends. We are silent in our camaraderie. I have secret friends, too—only the two of us know how close we are.

There's something about friendships that is difficult to pin down. It will not fit into a regular-sized box. It is magical. It happens by itself. Sometimes we find it so uneasy that we make it un-happen.

There are stages in our life when friends and family don't mix. We protect our parents from finding out too much about the people we hang out with. Most of my friends were useless when our babies were babies. Don't even get me started on the dynamic between friends and the spouse—let's just say, they take a while to accept the competition.

'Hello, friend-in-law,' my friend Rachana says to my husband, reminding him that she had me before he came along.

Some friends are always there. Some, less so. At times, we have to let a few go. We need time off; perhaps they need it, too.

I dream of the friends I have lost to the world. Some

return with a new voice, a new lilt to their drawl. They pass judgement, yet I find them adorable. Some return younger than before. They plug the gaps in my own life.

Friends do come back. Life is long.

All my friends are alcoholics, I once wrote in my diary. It's a theme in my friendships—to discover a pattern of addiction in each other's family history. These friends are incredible at offering and seeking support. They are wise, intuitive and funny. We heal together.

You know you are doing well when there is together-time with family, alone-time with yourself, and then, there are friends.

Friends nurture us. Their swear words liberate us. The mockery they make of us is refreshing. Their guffaw is all we need to banish the silence in our lives.

What Does It Take to Be Nineteen Again?

'Think of yourself as the sky,' she said to me. 'Everything else is a cloud. Coming and going in different shapes and colours. They pass. You stay.'

When I first got to know Rachana in college, what struck me was that she was a great laugher. There, I made up a word for her. 'Laugher!' Her laugh was giggly and full of abandon. She was more reckless than me on any ordinary day but was smart enough to know when to wind down and hit those psychology textbooks. I almost felt betrayed when our exam results were announced. I was jealous of how well she fared.

You're not really a friend of mine until I am jealous of you. It's not petty jealousy, it's pretty serious business. When my friends WhatsApp me photos from their holidays, award functions and other adventures, I mutter cuss-words under my breath. Then I type 'wow, too cool' into the chat window.

Rachana had been away in Washington, DC for two decades and had recently returned home to Kathmandu. She visited me in New Delhi and, as luck would have it, our other friends from college weren't in town. I had Rachana all to myself.

We were nineteen again. Or so I thought—until I went to pick her up from her cousin's home and her niece came to the door. That's Rachana, I thought to myself as I looked at the nineteen-year-old college student. Then, my friend Rachana appeared from behind her.

'We really have become aunts,' I admitted to her as she got into the car. She giggled.

We had met at her home in the US once when both of us had just started working. We had sat up all night exchanging notes on the fate of our college romances and our broken hearts. We were still trying to figure out love. We wondered how we would know when true love arrived.

We lost each other for many years after that. Our phone numbers changed, we got busy and distracted. Our new love lives were as complex as before, but less carefree. I would google her name and university to see if I could find her.

She tells me now that she had searched for me on the Doordarshan website and we collapse with laughter again.

'For god's sake, Rachana, I was with NDTV!'

'La,' she replies, 'I knew you were with TV.'

Rachana is Nepali. She speaks an adorable brand of Hindi because she went to school in Kalimpong, West Bengal, and then practised it with Delhi autowallahs and Sarojini Nagar salesmen when she was studying in Delhi University with me.

'Do you remember how you used to forge your mother's signature all the time?' she asks me in front of my children, as we relax with cups of tea in my home.

'Whaaaa?' I reply. 'When? What for?'

'Your mother was my local guardian. You used to sign the form every weekend to get me out of the girls' hostel.'

'I learnt to imitate Mom's signature in school. It was easy. My father's signature is much too complex,' I admit sheepishly to my children.

I remind Rachana of her flattering denim skirt with the slit at the back and her adventures in it at the St Stephen's bus stop. She pretends she has forgotten about it. More giggles.

I have no intention of mellowing in life. Maybe I am mellower now but I fully expect to return to my pre-mellow ways as soon as I can afford to stop being wise and responsible all the time.

Years after our meeting in her US home, Rachana had got in touch with me when she belatedly joined Facebook. She greeted me with scanned photos of us on our college campus. We were simultaneously jubilant and embarrassed. There we were being ragged on Fresher's Day. In our oversized clothes and ambitious haircuts, and with small, unlined faces.

I scanned through her Facebook albums. She had a Buddhist teacher. She meditated and went on pilgrimages. She had trained as a therapist. She was healing herself and learning to be a healer.

Back in India, as she pottered around in my home in her pyjamas and we caught up on stories, the dots began to connect. She told me dramatic tales from her childhood for the first time. We talked about caste and religion and cultural conflicts. She sat with my daughters and I watched them share selves with her in ways I had never seen before.

My family got a glimpse of a lighter, naughtier me. Rachana taught Aliza and me a technique to de-stress quickly when agitated. I got a chance to practise it soon enough. It worked!

'I'm glad you made your marriage work,' she said. 'I mean it in a good way.' She giggled again.

'I know what you mean,' I replied.

As we talked, we were back in our own bubble. Twenty years later, it was easy to tell what had brought us together in college.

We didn't take a single photo of the two of us together. We didn't need one.

"Oh okay," she figures.
"Pradesh is like a surname.
Himachal Pradesh,
Uttar Pradesh,
Madhya Pradesh ... like
everyone in a family has the
same name."

Recovering the Idea of India

This is a story of horror and hope. I've been meaning to tell it for a while, but self-doubt is a big bully. Today, I remind myself—people who listen to stories understand a lot more about the nuances in them than those who narrate them—

In November 1996, I was in a television studio late at night when there was a news flash that two aeroplanes had crashed into each other mid-air near Delhi. There was a sense of complete disbelief that gave way to shock as the news was confirmed. One of the planes was a passenger airline flying to Saudi Arabia and the other was from Kazakhstan. Both planes had crashed into the ground in the fields near Charkhi Dadri, a village 100 kilometres west of New Delhi.

We had just finished recording the last news bulletin of the day. Prannoy Roy had anchored the show. In comparison to the strength of the newsroom at daytime, only a handful of us were still around, finishing our edits and working on scripts.

A few hours later, just after midnight, my colleagues, Radhika and Kanan, and I walked over the wreckage, trying to get as close as possible to the fire that still raged after the collision. In the darkness, I stumbled upon the first dead body that I had ever seen in my life at close quarters. I switched on the battery-operated light mounted on my camera. A man was lying on his back, his body still fresh in death. I began to frame shots of him. In a desperate bid to concentrate, I carried forth an internal dialogue, directing my actions as a cameraperson—take a full long shot of the body; a close mid-shot of the face; focus on the details of that bloody, bruised hand. I was a solitary witness to the man's death. It would be hours, maybe days, until his family would receive the news of his tragic fate.

I was a woman at work.

There was a lot of commotion in the distance. All news crews began rushing in one direction. We followed. Videographers and journalists were now walking backwards over debris and bodies, trying to get shots and collect a sound byte from the first VIP to arrive. Walking firmly towards the wildly beating fire was the grandson of a powerful politician, surrounded with his entourage.

'What brings you here?' reporters asked him.

'Just plain curiosity,' he smiled. 'Did you get that?' he repeated. 'Plane curiosity!'

I was disgusted. Kanan and I continued to take more shots. With the heavy tripod strapped to his shoulder, Kanan guided me through the darkness—both of us avoiding stepping over broken luggage, passports, bodies of people fallen from the sky.

We went to the hospital in the village closest to the crash site. Bodies had been lined in rows in the open corridor. There was the unbearable smell of charred flesh. I recognized a man in mourning. He was the librarian from the media institute where I had been a postgraduate student. He was inconsolable. His brother was dead.

We sent tapes back to our office by the car we had come

in. Dawn broke. We saw our colleagues filming the debris from a helicopter to get an exclusive aerial view.

I felt angry, looking up from the ground. All 349 people aboard both the flights had died in the collision.

We were exhausted. After a long dark night, the morning unveiled the real scale of the disaster. Other news crews began to arrive from our office to relieve us.

As we left, we saw a sea of people ambling through the fields towards the crash site. Many of them from the villages in the vicinity had never seen an aeroplane up close before. They were coming to see the spectacle. We could have been in the middle of any Indian festival.

We had exclusive footage. Videos shot by us were bought by news agencies and channels from across the world. In the newsroom there was an air of jubilation that disaster reporting always seems to bring with it.

The smell of burnt flesh would linger around me for days after I returned from Charkhi Dadri. I would bathe many times over and I would still be able to sense that acrid smell in the air. I may have gone numb, but the odour pressed against my skin. I put away the shoes that had inadvertently trampled over the dead.

Among the passengers on the two flights, had been migrant workers from Uttar Pradesh and Bihar en route to Saudi Arabia. The families of many of the the dead did not know the details of their itinerary. There were bodies that remained unrecognized. There were body parts that did not fit.

Two weeks later, I went to film in the hospital morgue in

Delhi where the unclaimed had been preserved. It was time to perform the last rites. Sealed wooden caskets were loaded on to tempos. We began to take shots with our cameras. A large rat crawled out of one of the coffins as my camera began rolling. I held my breath. It was that stench again.

Two organizations—one affiliated with Islam and another with Hinduism—had stepped in to perform the rituals that go with death. I followed a van that was transporting some of the bodies to a graveyard near Feroz Shah Kotla Fort in Delhi. I had never been to a burial ground before. I was the only woman in the crowd. Everyone made place for me as I began filming.

Bodies in white shrouds were lowered into freshly dug graves. Some sheets just held isolated anatomical parts. The slanting light of dusk washed over us as a group of men began to recite verses from the Quran. I took a shot of a man throwing a fistful of loose earth over a stranger's body. The image of the actor Amitabh Bachchan burying his loved ones in a film flashed before my eyes. It gave me solace. It made the scene I was a part of familiar.

All of us left the graveyard together and drove straight to a cremation ground in Safdarjung Enclave. Up until then, I hadn't realized how syncretic the group of volunteers had been.

At the Hindu cremation ground, the solemn faces of young Muslim men with skull caps stood out visually. Many pyres were set alight together. I zoomed in to take close-ups of the volunteers standing on the other side of the rising flames. Everyone in white, the pandit and the maulvi, side by side, paying their respects to those unknown.

My tears began to flow. There was much to mourn. I returned to office, handed over the tapes for editing and broke down in the bathroom, letting out sobs that had been stuck for days.

Somewhere in that scene, there was a sort of redemption. Amidst the horror of the deaths, I had also witnessed a tangible idea of India—of our shared identity, our humanity.

Papa As the Nation I Know

As I spoke to my father-in-law, everyone in the family grew quiet, almost tense.

It was the first time Papa was visiting our home in Delhi and I got a moment with him only when we were already on our way to the railway station to drop him back. 'Did you enjoy yourself, Papa?' I asked from the back seat of the car. Ammi smiled uncomfortably at the silliness.

'Papa does not enjoy himself in our company,' his daughter finally said. 'He just puts up with us somehow. He will be back in his element when he reaches his home in the village.'

'No, I think Papa looks quite happy,' I said, refusing to accept her version of him over my version of him. 'Tell me, Papa?' I asked again.

'Yes, I enjoyed myself,' he said from the front seat of the car.

'Come again soon and stay with us.'

'Let me leave first. Then we shall see,' he said.

Of all the Papas I have known, my husband's father is the gentlest, kindliest of them all, with small eyes that twinkle when he smiles.

Mirza Ashfaq Beg was a seventeen-year-old student in 1947 when India was divided to create Pakistan. His elder brother worked as a customs officer in Chittagong (now in Bangladesh). He chose to hold on to his job and thus, his family and he became Pakistanis. Papa went to study at Aligarh Muslim University and became a lecturer in an intermediate college in Ghazipur in eastern Uttar Pradesh. He retired from the same institution as the principal.

When we travel in the villages and towns near his home, we invariably meet someone who recognizes us as the family of 'Principal Sahab'. His students are everywhere. We are treated to stories of Papa's glory. For forty years, he was re-elected as the gram pradhan of his village panchayat; he is widely respected as a leader of the community.

'I did not know who my father was till I travelled with him on his campaign trail,' Afzal had told me once. Papa had been a candidate in the 2002 legislative elections in Uttar Pradesh. His speeches, laced with Urdu poetry, would draw large crowds—but they failed to get him many votes.

'He is a very good man, he has done so much for us, but you see, *politics mein sharafat ki koi jagah nahi hai*—there is no space in politics for civility,' people would say.

Krishnanand Rai, the candidate who was elected from the same constituency, was shot dead in an ambush three years later, allegedly by assailants hired by his political rivals. I was in the newsroom at work when the headlines broke. My hands went cold with dread. In my own way, I realized the importance of Papa losing that election.

When his wife—my mother-in-law—died, my friend Aneela sent me a cryptic message. 'Which one of you will become Ammi now, that is the question.'

We discovered that the answer to Aneela's question was Papa. He seemed to have decided that no one was going to feel Ammi's loss as long as he could help it. He began to fuss over everyone, worry about travel schedules, and order favourite food items for each person in the family. His own grown children marvelled at this side of his personality—unfamiliar, as they were, to seeing him as the nurturing parent.

Papa's children and extended family take him very seriously as the patriarch. He is surrounded by people trying to anticipate his needs.

The first person who smashed this hierarchy was Papa's youngest grandchild—our daughter Naseem. In a house full of people, she would toddle up to her grandfather with her shoes in her hand and ask him to help her wear them and tie her shoelaces. She would insist that only he could read stories to her from her books. Ammi would laugh with embarrassment at the scene.

This is the only version of Papa that Naseem and I have ever known, and for us, this kind, attentive grandparent is his essential self.

Almost fifteen years after that first conversation with Papa in the car, he is staying with us again, as he recovers from a spinal fracture and other illnesses. I hold and caress his hand a lot, consoling both of us at the same time. It is time for us to care for those who have taken care of others all their lives.

While I manage the logistics of home, hospitals, schools and work, his son and grandson have been his primary caregivers. Often, they retreat from his room, unable to feed or convince him in the way they hope. Papa gets frustrated, even scolds them on occasion.

When I enter the room, he always smiles, no matter how feeble he may be feeling. 'Don't be anxious,' he says to me. 'How are the children? Take care of yourself.'

'Papa, have some soup with a slice of bread,' I say. He agrees with a nod.

For once, I am the good cop and my husband is the bad cop of the family. I love this privilege.

When Afzal and I got married, Ammi and Papa had hosted a lavish wedding reception, a walima, in their village home. Over three days, approximately 5,000 people from surrounding villages attended the feast.

Papa had got our wedding cards printed in Urdu, Hindi and English, with my parents' Hindu names next to his own Muslim name.

This man, lying sick in bed, is the India I was born in. He is the India that I care to live in—an India that honours my choices and meets me where I am; that listens to each opinion; that reinvents itself to make place for my children.

'What is the news?' he asks me, as his pain subsides. I don't tell him about a viral video depicting a brutal assault on African students within a kilometre of where we live. I don't mention anti-Romeo squads humiliating young people in parks and streets in his beloved Uttar Pradesh. I don't bring up the controversies over the Finance Bill amendments.

I hold his hand in mine, searching for something to say.

Love in the Times of Jihad

These days I call myself a Love Jihadi. It amuses me no end.

A while ago, my husband was at the local electricity office, trying to convince the officers to restore power supply at the factory space he oversees.

'We cannot come in the way of nation-building,' he said to them, trying to present a case they would not be able to argue against. 'You and I must contribute to this collective goal. Restoring electricity in our factory is a duty . . . to safeguard the country's economic growth.'

He turned to look at me and make sure that I was playing the role of an important-looking-media-walli who must not be messed with. I was distracted. 'I'm just a love jihadi,' I thought to myself, but I quickly tried to look stern and cross at the same time.

These days, our children are learning to read Arabic over weekends. They made good progress in the early weeks but then, it seemed, their heart wasn't in it.

'Tell them stories,' I requested their teacher. 'They like stories.'

Last Saturday, my daughters began to tell me the tale of Prophet Musa and King Fir'aun.

'The king had a dream that a baby boy would be born who would grow up and kill him,' said one.

'Just like King Kansa of Mathura,' I added, excited. 'He was the uncle of Krishna.'

'King Fir'aun ordered that all newborn boys get killed.

So Musa's parents put him in a basket and set him afloat—across the River Nile—to save his life.'

'Just like Krishna! I mean like Karna,' I said. It was fascinating. After this I behaved myself, stopped interrupting and listened to the story quietly—my eyes big like saucers.

The year Afzal and I got married, both of us had witnessed the aftermath of the riots in Gujarat. It was the summer of 2002. He had gone to volunteer in the refugee camps in Ahmedabad after I had returned from a work assignment there.

My friends Barkha, Rachna and I had been filming in Vadodara when a group of people drove up in a Honda City car. A young woman in her early twenties said she had been looking for us ever since she had heard that our news team had arrived in the city. She wanted us to visit her home.

Ayesha's neighbourhood was the equivalent of Delhi's Greater Kailash 1. Her house had been set ablaze by rioters. Parts of the floor were still so hot that it was not entirely safe to venture beyond the threshold. I took careful steps, my video camera balanced on my hip, observing the remains of a home—a charred refrigerator, a heap of ash where the dining table had been. I remember the shoes I was wearing as I stepped over the rubble, filming the devastation. Barkha was talking to Ayesha and some other people in her family. There was a wrought-iron swing in the lawn. I touched it cautiously. That swing was life—their life as it had been.

In November 1984, my brothers and I had stood on the roof of our DDA flat in New Delhi to witness a mob setting fire to a newly whitewashed house in Panchsheel Enclave.

The place had been looted the night before and the Sikh family had fled. For years I used to peer from the window of my school bus, staring at the ruined home. The fire had inked dark patterns on the walls outside. What did it mean to lose your home like this?

'They won't come back,' my brother had explained to me. 'They will probably sell this place for whatever it is worth.'

Our hearts break and somehow they keep working. Lives are wrecked and people get back to building homes again. We lose hope and then we find a way to believe once more. We often despair that we are too cynical but we are all constantly creating, restoring, healing, trying to reassemble broken pieces.

The first time I began to have a conversation with our firstborn about why we were celebrating Eid, even though her school was not, she interrupted me: 'I know, Mamma. Prateeksha told me.'

'What did she say?'

'She said, "I am a Pandit, you are a Muslim."'

'Excellent,' I thought to myself. 'Good job, Prateeksha.'

It's crazy when you look at events in isolation. We are taught to recognize differences. Love is hated. Hate is loved. If I can hate vocally and violently, I'm in. If I convey my love, I must stand outside the classroom and reflect on what I've done wrong; such acts can get me expelled.

Love jihadis are sneaky. They are experts at love. They can adore you even if you insist on hating them.

After our visit to the electricity supply office, my husband took me to the local police station. He needed to file an

FIR to report a missing power metre. Sometimes we flirt with each other and refer to these chores as dates. We have three small children, you see—we must appreciate the little time we get together, alone.

'I'm a journalist,' I practised softly a few times—just in case I needed to whip out the sentence to inspire people to do the work they were being paid to do anyway. We must have looked menacing enough because the paperwork got done smoothly. I stared at a man sitting on his haunches in the corner of the police station. His wrists had been tied together with a jute rope. He had been caught and caged.

'I want to go to the temple,' I said to my husband as we walked out of the police station. Instead of getting into our parked car, we crossed the road to enter a swanky new Jain temple.

My seven-year-old daughter's words echoed in my head as I walked into the inner sanctum: 'Mamma, can we go to a temple even if we don't pray?'

"My Ma'am only rewards speed. She understands slow and fast. She doesn't understand good and bad. And she never notices good hand-writing," she says.

"It's the breaking news model," I reply.

Yes, I Am a Pakistani

'Are you a Pakistani?'

The first time I overheard this question, our firstborn child was five years old. We were attending a pre-wedding function at a friend's home. It was late November 2008, and ten terrorists from Pakistan had laid siege to Mumbai with a series of coordinated shootings and bombings. Staff and guests of the Taj Mahal Palace Hotel were still trapped in a hostage crisis and rescue operations were being covered live on 24X7 news channels across India. Almost everyone at the wedding function discussed the unfolding events. Besides the hundreds of injured, 166 people would die in this attack.

'What is your name?' an older child asked my daughter.

'Sahar,' she answered.

'Are you a Pakistani?' asked the child.

I gasped involuntarily but I held myself back from jumping into their conversation.

'No,' said my daughter. 'Aiman is a Pakistani. I am from Greater Noida.'

I didn't need to rescue my child from this 'slur' just yet. It was but a tiny misunderstanding that she had to clear.

Aiman's mother is my husband's elder sister. By extension, Aiman is Sahar's older cousin who lives in Karachi and visits us in India regularly. Aiman is also my children's heroine. Sahar wrote about her in an essay in school.

Aiman is my best friend. She wears jeans and T-shirts and doesn't like wearing skirts. My mother says I learnt to eat potato chips from her. Aiman loves to cycle very fast in her colony and has many pet animals. She has rabbits, a cat, and fish in an aquarium. She has to keep the rabbits and fish safe from the cat.

In the summer of 2014, when schools on both sides of the India–Pakistan border were closed for vacations, Aiman visited us with her mother. My parents-in-law were hosting all their children and grandchildren in their home in east Uttar Pradesh. The adults scanned newspapers and sifted through headlines on their smartphones—there was political upheaval in New Delhi; heinous crimes against women were being reported from across the state. My father-in-law read editorials in three newspapers—one in English, another in Hindi, and a third in Urdu. He highlighted passages for me to discuss with him.

Litchis, mangoes and melons were peeled and cut. Children ran around us, playing hide-and-seek in the long afternoons—they were forbidden from going out in the sun. Someone would get hurt. A few were thirsty.

They settled down to choose a film from a USB drive an older cousin happened to be carrying. They wanted to watch *The Road to El Dorado*, but its format wasn't compatible with the DVD player in the house. I suggested *Sholay*.

'It has too much fighting and Amitabh Bachchan dies,' protested my daughter. That wasn't her definition of entertainment.

The only other film available was *Gandhi*—Richard

Attenborough's 1982 biopic. It may have just been a coincidence—but here was a group of children from Karachi, New Delhi and Lucknow watching *Gandhi* together in a village in Uttar Pradesh. I joined them. It had been years since I had watched *Gandhi*. I had been overwhelmed and inspired when I had seen it first as a twelve-year-old. Our school had booked an entire cinema hall for its students.

I explained events and scenes to the children as they unfolded on the screen.

'That's Nehru, that's Patel and that is Jinnah,' I said, the first time they appeared.

'Jinnah!' exclaimed Aiman. 'Quaid-e-Azam.'

The afternoon had come alive for Aiman. She noticed Jinnah in every scene. Sahar was too tense to watch the violence. She ran off to reread one of her Harry Potter books. Another child left the room as troops led by General Dyer began to march into Jallianwala Bagh in the film. The rest viewed the massacre in stunned silence. Hundreds of bodies piled up as soldiers shot relentlessly at unarmed people gathered for a protest meeting on Baisakhi. It was 13 April 1919 in Amritsar.

'I have been to Amritsar many times,' twelve-year-old Aiman said. When she travels between Lahore and New Delhi by bus, her mother always shops in Amritsar. They visit the Golden Temple, too.

The film drew to an end.

'After this, they will launch the Quit India Movement and then India will become independent,' I told the children, preparing them for scenes of more bloodshed. 'But there will also be Partition. India and Pakistan will become two separate countries.'

Aiman clapped her hands. 'Pakistan!'

I was startled at first and then I realized that this is where the child recognized her part of the story. I let go of my dismay, and began celebrating with her. My mother was four years old in 1947 when her extended family and she came to Amritsar as refugees from Lahore.

> When Aiman visits during her school holidays, she gets her holiday homework along with her. Her English books are just like mine. She studies Urdu and not Hindi like us. In her holiday homework, she writes about the things we do together. So do I.

The hours slipped away. It was close to midnight. This would be the last occasion for the cousins to be together. I was sitting in the covered verandah, while the children lay on folding beds arranged side by side on the open terrace. They had permission to stay awake for as long as they liked. I could hear them discussing the stars in the sky. On tippy-toes, my eight-year-old came to me and asked if it was possible for some stars to be moving.

'We see something red that is blinking,' she said.

'Maybe it's a shooting star,' I answered, quite sure I was giving her the wrong answer.

She returned to break the news to her cousins.

'Mamma, in this world there are many different worlds like India, America, Pakistan, but everywhere there is the same sky,' my youngest child informed me.

You May Say I'm a Dreamer

My husband Afzal was going to be in Amritsar for a night and I offered to book a room for him online. Besides the fact that I am a good person and like to be helpful, this also ensured that I could spend some time being online, without him accusing me of wasting my time on the Internet. My husband is an old-fashioned man who still believes that there is a boundary between the online and offline world. I, as you may know, like to see myself as being trendy, if not a trendsetter.

'Find me something old-world, something classy and charming in Amritsar,' he said.

'I doubt I will find anything like that in Amritsar,' I replied.

Unlike me, Afzal is not a realist. He can imagine anything anywhere.

I am not only practical, but I am also very efficient when I receive instructions. I found a homestay with an elegant website, photographs of luminous curtains, enchanting dark wood furniture and an aesthetic feel that was minimalistic—all of which made me think that this would be a very expensive place to book. I showed the photos to Afzal and no such thought occurred to him. He asked me to book it, and immediately began to fantasize about a second visit when all of us would stay together in those large rooms.

'People with homes of this sort probably don't like children occupying their property,' I told him. 'We will have to speak in whispers.'

The difference between Afzal and me is that he is a dreamer and I am khadoos—a grouch.

I dialled the number mentioned on the website and my call was answered by a very gracious, polite voice—by the woman who was the owner of the homestay. I spoke in my most courteous manner to match hers. She had grown children who had moved away and now there was this big house. The homestay ensured her husband and she had company every now and then, and the money that trickled in helped maintain the estate. I agreed with everything she said. We discovered common friends and nostalgic connections with Pondicherry and the Aurobindo Ashram. She told me of the room charges. She said my husband could pay when he arrived; a room would be ready for him.

'Money is not important, people are important,' she said.

'Yes, of course,' I replied.

She gave me the number of the caretaker who would answer the door if she wasn't there. Everything about our conversation was positive and warm. It offered the instant high that many online chats and phone exchanges do—when we seem to connect with strangers who reaffirm our faith.

Finally, as the conversation drew to a close, I mentioned my husband's name to her to confirm the booking.

After that, the lady stopped sounding very articulate. I wasn't quite sure what had happened as I hung up.

I dialled her number half an hour later and directly asked the question that troubled me. 'I felt some hesitation on your part before I ended our last call,' I said.

'No, it's not that,' she replied. 'I want you to make a full payment in advance via an online bank transfer.'

'Is there a problem because you heard a Muslim name?' I asked.

'We have to be careful, you know. My husband and I had some Muslim friends ourselves. It's not that we don't like Muslims. You know how the world is these days.'

She then told me an elaborate story about a Muslim woman who had come to stay as a guest, borrowed some money from her and later duped the family. She was concerned that she had to share information about her guests with the local police and she would have to answer awkward questions if Afzal stayed. She said that her husband wasn't well enough to take charge and she was worried.

I told her I would call her back. This is when I discovered the real difference between Afzal and me.

I narrated the episode to him. I told him that there was no reason to stay with people who regarded him with suspicion because they equated Muslims with terrorists and con men.

Afzal insisted that he would stay with this couple with a posh accent and an elegant house in Amritsar.

While I had immediately written them off, Afzal was sure that he wished to engage with them. Whereas I felt snubbed, he was calm. He told me to make the advance payment online. 'It is important for this woman to meet me, Natasha,' he said. 'What good will it do if we get offended and start fighting with people? How will we deal with those who are really dangerous if we don't face up to those who are our own?'

'Look, I will book you a really fancy room somewhere

else,' I said, now feeling rash enough to suppress the voice that said this move was a waste of money.

'This woman at the homestay needs to meet people like me,' Afzal argued. 'Trust me, I have studied in Tilak Dhari Singh Chhatri Inter College in Jaunpur . . . a senior school for upper-caste Hindu boys. I was the only Muslim in my batch. Boys would search for me just to see what I looked like. The son of the Vishwa Hindu Parishad leader in the city became my best friend. He took me under his wing to protect me. Eventually I became the favourite student of the teachers.'

'So you think this lady will see your beautiful face and twinkling eyes and feel better about the world?'

'Exactly,' he said. 'I'm sure she has a beautiful, antique porcelain tea set. I want to have tea with this couple. It will be charming.'

The difference between Afzal and me is that while I spend a lot of time worrying about the state of the world, this man always has a good cup of tea on his mind.

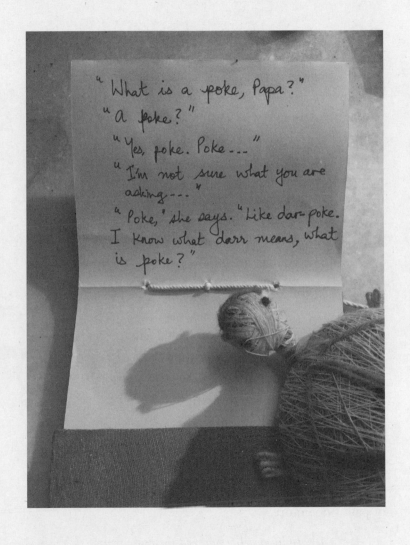

Saying Sorry to Shahrukh Khan

There is a song in *Chak De! India* that has an unexpected effect on me.

It happened first during a car journey. I had been travelling to the Tis Hazari District Courts with my three-year-old daughter by my side. We were going to be by the side of a friend who was fighting a bitter custody case in the family court. I was already emotional. Both parents are my friends and I have loved them dearly. Now I was being forced to choose a side in public. It was terrible to watch one of my friends—the father of the child—helplessly from a distance without being able to reach out to him. En route, a song from *Chak De! India* began playing in the car:

> *Teeja tera rang tha main toh,*
> *Jiya tere dhang se main toh,*
> *Tu hi tha maula, tu hi aan,*
> *Maula mere lele meri jaan [. . .]*
> *Tujh se hi rooth na re, tujhe hi manana,*
> *Tere mera naata koi dooja na jaana.*

Just like that tears started rolling down my cheeks. I couldn't understand why. We reached the court and spent the day trying to negotiate a bewildering and aggressive judicial system. Later, the song played in the car again. I felt pangs of pain once more.

> *I have lived a life adorned in your colours,*
> *I have lived my life by your rules,*

You were my god, you were my pride,
Take this life, dear lord, it's entirely yours. [. . .]
It's with you I argue, and with you I make up,
What we share is a secret, known only to us.

What memories were these words stirring? Who did I feel misunderstood by? And who did I want to make peace with? It took a while for the answers to emerge.

My parents are Punjabis. My mother was born in Lahore and grew up in Amritsar, close to the Golden Temple. For her, going to the temple was synonymous with visiting a gurdwara. Her Hanuman Chalisa lay next to her Sukhmani Sahib. There was plenty of space.

When we would travel from our childhood home in Ranchi, Bihar to visit family in Delhi and Punjab, we were called Biharis. 'Here come the rice-eating Biharis with their *ek tho, do tho, teen tho,*' our Mami would say. So we were Hindu-Sikh-Biharis.

When I grew up and travelled to Lahore, I tried to prepare myself for a brush with 'Muslim culture'. I was amazed to find myself in a vibrant Punjab, where I discovered my own urban Punjabi identity for the first time. Everyone spoke like my Mamajis. But of course! My uncles had been Lahoris. I became a Hindu-Sikh-Bihari-Lahori.

In Lahore, we had a taxi driver named Javed. He would pick us up from the Pearl Continental Hotel, admire our TV broadcasting equipment and watch us interview very important people. He took me to the best eateries, told me about his romances and, of course, shared his political insights regarding the state of the subcontinent. When it was time for us to return, Javed gave me some advice for my future: 'Be careful who you marry. Most men who woo you will probably do it for your money. Besides, I hear those Indian men beat their wives. Take care of yourself.'

I laughed out loud. The shock of this statement stayed with me for a long time. Especially because it brought home the latent bias that I had grown up with—that most Muslim men ill-treat their wives. We think we know it all till we discover that most of our knowledge is a truckload of biases—a way of hating the 'other' to avoid focusing on the trouble within.

My husband is a Muslim from Uttar Pradesh and our children, brought up in India's capital, have a combined Hindu-Sikh-Bihari-Lahori-Muslim-UP-Delhi heritage.

My grandfather would speak Punjabi with an Urdu accent. He read the Gita in Urdu every day. My father-in-law recites Persian poetry. My father speaks Hindi with a Punjabi accent and our children first spoke English with a Walt Disney lilt. In a way, this feels unique, but actually there is nothing extraordinary about any of this.

Our syncretic roots, combined with the choices we have made, give all of us a multi-dimensional identity.

Being singled out or facing discrimination for one or many of these identities is an equally common experience. Some of us deal with it by denying the existence of prejudices, others choose to express and share their dismay. Some forget many parts of their own identity in an attempt to assimilate; some confront the bigotry; others hide till it is safe to come out.

You don't need to be uprooted to know what homelessness feels like.

To lead a creative life, you often make the critical decision of not belonging. On the flip side, there is that inevitable longing to fit in—to belong in equal measure to both private worlds and the public ones outside.

In an essay on his life in *Outlook Turning Points*, published in association with the *New York Times*, Shahrukh Khan, the superstar-actor, wrote:

> I sometimes become the inadvertent object of political leaders who choose to make me a symbol of all that they think is wrong and unpatriotic about Muslims in India. I have been accused of bearing allegiance to our neighbouring nation rather than my own country. This, even though I am an Indian whose father fought for the freedom of India.

In the same essay he wrote about the Pathan identity he had inherited from his parents, his marriage to his Hindu wife Gauri, and how he answered the questions his children asked him about their identity—he sang them a song that at its core meant: Be a good human being, the rest will sort itself out.

What followed was a severe and abusive backlash. One columnist,, writing a think piece in an online publication, accused the actor of being ungrateful and thankless; mediocre and boorish. He added:

> Don't bite the hand that fed you—and made you who you are—by running off to an overseas publication and

crying your heart out, thereby providing space for low-life
terrorists like Hafiz Saeed to take pot-shots at India.

In essence, he implied: If you talk openly about being a
Muslim in India, we will mock you and call you a traitor.
Instead of standing up to terrorists who don't need a valid
excuse to take pot-shots, we will turn our venom towards
our own. We will not allow differences to get expressed. We
will silence you.

This shockingly coarse comment brought back the song
from *Chak De! India*. I found myself circling the same set of
questions: Who was this person in my life whose approval
was so important to me? Who was I willing to die for?

The answers came together like pieces of a puzzle. The
lyrics evoked the struggle to belong to one's homeland; to
society; to authority figures in our life who have rejected us
for the personal choices we have made.

In *Chak De! India*, Shahrukh Khan plays Kabir Khan,
the captain of the Indian hockey team. When the film
opens, India is playing against Pakistan in the finals of an
international tournament. As the match draws to a nail-
biting close, Kabir Khan fails to score a goal with a penalty
stroke. India loses and various television news channels are
quick to accuse the Muslim captain of the team of having
sold his soul to Pakistan. In the film, a photograph of Kabir
Khan shaking hands with the captain of the Pakistani hockey
team is used manipulatively to prove that he has betrayed
the trust of his country. His career ends all too abruptly
and, humiliated, he is forced to move out of his ancestral
home. A passionate sportsman is punished for being a Khan.

In a statement to the press clarifying what he had written for *Outlook Turning Points*, Shahrukh Khan said:

> I am an actor and maybe I should just stick to stuff that all of you expect me to have a viewpoint on. The rest of it . . . maybe I don't have the right kind of media atmosphere to comment on. So I will refrain from it.

Come on, I wanted to tell the actor, that's not fair at all. Tell us your stories, Shahrukh Khan. Speak from your heart. Bullies are cowards, their words are empty shells.

When confronted on a show called *The Social Network* on NDTV, the columnist who had accused Shahrukh Khan admitted that he had commented about the actor's essay without having read the entire piece. As he presented his own defence, the columnist revealed how low the standards of journalism have fallen. He had triggered an abusive uproar against Shahrukh Khan on social media—without even bothering to read his words in their context.

On the show he had another chance to redeem himself and undo some of the hurt he had caused. He could have started by saying 'sorry'. He didn't.

Can Aliza's Idea of India Survive?

'I am a Muslim, a Hindu, an Indian and I love Harry Potter.'

I found this on the back page of my daughter's rice-paper diary when she was eight. She had put all the significant parts of herself together to define herself. It was an eight-year-old's one-line bio.

Two years later, Aliza was in a beauty salon, getting a haircut, when the hairstylist noticed her name and asked her if she was a 'Mohammedan'.

Aliza did not understand the question. She looked at me to ask what he meant.

'He is asking if you are a Muslim,' I said to her.

Aliza looked up at him in the mirror and nodded a yes.

Seven-year-old Naseem felt the need to elaborate. 'We are Hindu and Muslim,' she said.

'You cannot be both. You can be one of the two,' said the hairstylist.

'But we are,' said Naseem. 'Mamma, we are both Hindu and Muslim, right?' She turned to me for confirmation.

'You cannot be both,' he repeated.

'Maybe in your family you cannot, but in our family we can,' I told him. 'We can be whatever we choose to be.'

'Are you Muslim?' he asked me directly.

I wanted to stay calm. If my children detected anger, or heard my voice strain, they would know there was a brewing conflict.

To his credit, the hairstylist gave Aliza a really good haircut. It is unlikely that we will visit his salon again.

The next morning, Kanta, who works in our home, brought the morning newspaper to me. There was a photo of crying, grieving, screaming women on the front page. Kanta wanted me to read out the news to her.

'This is in Dadri, Kanta,' I said. 'It is your neighbourhood.'

'I know,' replied Kanta. 'It happened last night.'

'A mob lynched a man in his own home because they suspected there was beef in his refrigerator. His son is in hospital.'

We were alone at home. Kanta is a sensitive and loving person, and I was almost relieved that I didn't have to keep this news bottled up inside me.

'But, Bhabhi, they killed a calf,' said Kanta.

'It was a rumour.'

'No, it wasn't,' Kanta's voice rose. 'A calf was stolen in the middle of the night.'

'But you cannot kill a man so brutally even if he did kill a calf.' My frustration made me sound like I was yelling.

'It was a bachhra, Bhabhi,' she repeated. 'A calf!' To her mind, this justified everything.

I got up and walked out of the house. What was the point of directing my hostility towards Kanta? If I had been among my own family and friends—among people I otherwise respected for their intellect and empathy—I would still have heard the same tone-deaf responses disguised as analysis.

I walked into the park next to my home. Young men from the local Rashtriya Swayamsevak Sangh shakha come here every morning to exercise. From the voices that rise and drop, it seems as though the youngest amongst them bellows instructions and slogans into the dark morning air.

'Bharat Mata Ki Jai. Vande Mataram.'

The RSS routine coincides with the time my husband and I wake up to receive our yoga teacher in our home at dawn. Sometimes, we go for a walk in the park after yoga. The boys look just like the cousins and friends I grew up with. I wonder if I look familiar and friendly to them, too.

A friend called me in a state of agitation. 'What is the worst that can happen in this country?' she asked rhetorically.

I live less than 10 kilometres from Dadri, where Mohammad Akhlaq and his family were accused of slaughtering a cow and attacked by a murderous mob. A sewing machine from their own home was used as a weapon to bludgeon Akhlaq to death. His son Danish had to have multiple brain surgeries in a hospital. An older son Sartaj is an officer in the Indian Air Force.

My friend's question came back to me in another form. *What is the worst they can do to my family and me? What will I do when a mob comes towards my home?*

I felt ashamed of my paranoia. Yet, my brain, by default, was stacking up plans. In case of an emergency, what would our strategy to survive be? Who would we call? Where could we hide? Could we escape from the back of my house?

Ashok, who works as a driver for my family, is also from Kanta's village. He brought me versions of what really happened at the crime scene much before I began to read about it in the news. There had been no cow slaughter. Only the slaughter of a man.

At first, I decided I wouldn't talk about this incident

in front of my children. I was grateful that my husband was travelling so we could deal with our shock and pain in separate spaces.

But this wasn't just another incident of mob violence. Something intangible, yet precious had shattered. As a nation, we were standing in the midst of debris and rubble. As politicians, leaders and people continued to react and respond to what had happened, a dystopia revealed itself.

I eventually allowed Aliza and her sisters to overhear my conversations with Ashok as he described the brutality of the mob. Aliza read the rest of it in the front pages of the newspapers that I had left untouched.

Ashok reassured me that it would not happen to us. 'It is all vote politics,' he said. 'They need to consolidate the Hindu vote, so they are demonizing Muslims.'

I remembered Aliza's words on the back page of her diary. A Muslim, a Hindu, an Indian and a citizen of the world— our multiple identities do not diminish us, they create us.

Will Aliza's India survive? I know that my child's own version of her identity and where she belongs stands contaminated.

This page in her diary will fade with time. I take a photo to hold on to it.

"Will you still love me when you are twenty-eight?" I ask the child.

"Of course, Mamma!"

- Pause -

"Mamma, is it possible to fall out of love with one's own Mamma?"

"No, it isn't."

When Did You Last Go Home?

We returned home from the airport at 3 am. We were back from our holiday in Goa. Aliza had just turned one. She woke up as we entered our house, leapt out of my arms, ran to her room, pulled out her toys, touched the walls, and rolled on the floor. She was awake for a few hours, in communion with her world, her space in this world. A toddler was celebrating her homecoming.

I have an un-rooted, homeless vagabond inside me.

As a parent I am struck by our children's natural affinity for home. When our firstborn was an infant, home was us. She woke up with us, and slept only when we did. We bathed, nursed, and changed her diapers in hotel rooms, railway stations, boats, bus stands and roadside dhabas. Aliza, the second child, adopted the physical home as the centre of her universe. Our third child would create a home for all of us, bringing us all together. She'd own her world. I would watch her and learn.

I have always had trouble with belonging and fitting in. In retrospect, it doesn't seem like a bad thing at all. Not belonging anywhere helped me to accept everywhere. Having to adapt has taught me to adapt. Besides, I ask myself, how can I even imagine fitting in comfortably in a world full of injustice and war, torture, rape, genocide and dead children; in homes rife with suppressed hurt and unexpressed love?

Homes fascinate us. We look behind curtains and study the details of bathrooms. We peep into kitchens and look for stories on the shelves. We study photos online and try to imagine life outside the frame. Homes we have visited stay with us.

I have a visual memory of sitting on the kitchen counter at Khanna Aunty's, getting my nails painted. I was allowed to take as many cookies as I liked from her glass jar—she's dead now. Her life ended tragically. Moments of generosity stay with us.

I remember visiting a friend's home as a college student, where the table was laid with a Corning dinner set. I was amazed to see the familiar design—my parents had a similar dinner set that they had kept in a wall-mounted display unit for decades. I inherited it from them when I got married. We use it every day.

Another friend lived in a two-room barsati, which came with a beautiful wall with mud art, painted by his mother, a single parent. Crisp baingan slices fried with a thin coat of besan on them. A silent, brooding brother in the other room.

There are homes where everyone seems to be yelling, yet they burst into laughter a lot. There are polite homes, where the warmest welcome comes from the domestic staff. There are homes where everyone lives in a different home. Sometimes, fathers and sons do that. One enters, the other leaves. There are monologues, not conversations.

I have an inexplicable urge to go home, says my friend, trying to place her finger on the emotion. *I'm not sure where I want to go.* Home is where you go back to remember why you left home in the first place. Home is where Mum waits for you. Home is where Mum waits for you to leave again.

One of my best homes was my first workplace. When

I quit thirteen years later, there was one clear sentence in my head—'I just want to go home.' I was ready to grow up. I was ready for a new address. To reach where I was meant to belong, I had to un-belong elsewhere.

I hate being home. I also insist on being home. There's something or someone here that I am mending my relationship with. We need this time.

The big, fat family wants you to belong; the great system out there wants to own you. There's no need to oblige. You're not a cog in the wheel. Protect your talents, use them for free, it isn't necessary to set a price to everything.

We decorate our homes, we feel proud of them, we take photos when the light is just right. Sometimes we still don't feel at home. Something isn't okay in the expression in our eyes. We need to refresh our relationship, clean out the darkness and clutter.

Home is where you return after you are defeated. It takes defeat to find out what home is for. Home is where you recover. Where you have the permission to be ill. Silent. Messy. To own your resources.

I'm getting there. I'm not in a hurry. We need years of patience to reach a place of comfort.

Sometimes, I let the physical home wait. So many other things need ironing and fixing and nurturing. And neglecting. There's children, family, friends and me. Our work.

When your new voice is more powerful than the old nag inside you, you won't need to put yourself down any more. When you stop judging yourself, you find yourself at home. No more apologies, you are ready to be you.

Five Lessons I Learnt All by Myself

As any candid child or honest adult will tell you, being out and about in the world is often a cakewalk in comparison to being home with family. I showed this sentence to my twelve-year-old daughter and asked her if she thought it was accurate. She laughed out loud. 'Yes, Mamma, sometimes this is true,' she said. Encouraged by her kind endorsement, I shall share with you five unexpected lessons I have learnt all by myself, ever since I embarked on the family project as an adult.

There is a terrible person inside you

You are going to discover what a monster you are. You will yell at your little children when you are alone with them. You will not bathe for days. You will throw tantrums that only your kids will witness. You will try to pretend that such explosions are small things. Your children will bring this up a few years later as the worst memory of their childhood. They will repeat it many times over.

Listen to them. Apologize to them. They will look like they are not ready to let go of the episode. Don't become angry all over again. Show them that you can accept how they feel. Love is humility.

You will be a terrible person again. Your only protection is your ability to acknowledge this.

You cannot keep up with a fast-changing world

We are duffers. We thought we would ride the waves of change much better than our parents did—but the world proved us wrong by changing even more rapidly.

The world confuses us by dumbing down when we expected it to smarten up.

It is amazing how sluggish our brains become. Laugh at your ineptness. Buy your bruised ego an ice cream. Let your children run about and express themselves in their spaces without making them feel guilty about it. Ask them for help—it's the fringe benefit of having children.

Everything takes way more time than you had imagined

The baby is born and there is a momentary feeling of accomplishment. The first forty days and nights seem like a year. Baby learns to support her head. She sits up independently. She is ready to walk into pre-school. She gets busy exploring the room. You walk back—each minute spinning in slow motion—feeling like the greatest work you ever started in your life is now done.

You discover it isn't. Independence and dependence are like day and night on a rotating planet. And everything takes years, even decades, longer than you thought it would. It is astounding. It breaks you now and then. After every celebration is over, the real work starts. And it never finishes.

This is the way we stay alive.

Words are broken bridges

Everyone is feeling the same set of emotions. But we just don't seem to have a language to share our feelings—our version of our lives. We are terrified of listening to voices that validate our fears and inadequacies. We try to shut out, muzzle and unfollow comments that seem to reveal us.

Words do not always connect us to the other side. Sometimes, we find other ways to get across. Sometimes, we find that staying right here, on *this* side, is necessary and correct.

Aloneness is underrated

It takes a lot of relearning for many of us to accept the help of extended family, domestic staff, professionals and the community at large. On the flip side, I discovered a whole new meaning to the concept of 'alone time'. It is the most unacknowledged need across ages.

'Now you are all alone,' an older relative will comment on the phone after the guests have left.

'No, we are all together,' I will say.

'Yes, but you are alone,' she will say, as if that is not okay at all.

'We are together,' I will repeat to myself.

There are times when one of you will be travelling and away from home.

'Now you are all alone,' your neighbour will tell you.

'The children and I are together,' you will say.

'Yes, yes, all alone,' he will say.

'No, no, all together,' you will say.

There will be times when the rest of the family will leave and you will be at home.

'Oh no, you are all alone,' everyone will say with extreme concern.

'Yes! Yes, I am alone,' you will respond with happiness. 'I am alone. I am together.'

Footnotes and Endnotes

The title is deliberate. It's meant to distract everyone except those who like little notes.

This is really just a shiny new piece composed of leftover advice—the kind of thing that might call out to you in a flea market full of useful-looking useless things. If you stop, you will find yourself staying longer than you meant to, and then you might end up taking home something that doesn't seem to fit with the rest of your classy stuff. Don't blame me later.

Make friends. New friends. Waste lots of time talking, chatting, texting, sharing, commenting—and being silly. Sustain friendships that nurture the inner crazy and make you laugh unnecessarily. Friends are the family you choose. They keep you young.

Fight with your spouse. Make sure you fight in front of the children. Put up good fights. You don't want your children to grow up and not know how to frame a spectacular argument, or look authority in the eye, or stand up for themselves. Fight—and then always move on.

Being a role model is hard work. Fake it till you get it right.

Make a list of everything you don't want to do.

Make a list of everything you never wanted to be. Negative lists are full of power. There's not much left to do after the list is made. Day's work done. Take these lists very seriously. Hidden behind the things you never wanted will be *something*—I can't say what—it's your list, you will find it.

Stay focused on all that is useless for a week. I'm doing that now.

'Bhabhi,' Kanta Mausi, who cooks for us, calls me from the kitchen. Naseem, the boss in the house, laughs out loud.

'Mamma is not Barbie,' she says, covering her mouth with her hands.

'Whatever you say, Naseem,' says Kanta Mausi. 'You know best.'

Collect your silly moments.

It takes three to make a marriage. A couple and a home. Or a couple and a car. Or maybe their playlist.

Recognize the moments that are yours. Create cozy corners for yourselves as a couple, the way you did when you were new lovers—not physical spaces, but small intimacies that everyone can see but no one else can recognize. Like teatime, for example. Quick tea, elaborate tea, tea followed by another cup of tea, impromptu tea, tea in new places, unexpected spaces, tea on the train. I don't even like tea, but I love the excuse to do nothing together.

I have an older brother I crave to talk to. He calls regularly. Before I can start saying something, he places the phone against his son's ear. 'Talk to Bhua,' he says. He has three children. It will be a while before he borrows the phone to speak to me directly. We have learnt to chat on messaging apps. It is here that he will tell me what is on his mind. I reassure him. He sends me confidence. We share stories and jokes about our lives. This is how my brother does conversations with me.

Keep talking. Keep calling and writing. Start texting

people who claim they never check their messages or don't know how to. Maybe it's because no one sends them any. What are we doing on social networks, anyway? We practise friendship. We also practise love and anger. We get really good at some of it. Then we bring it all home. *Why don't you go away so I can text you*, I sometimes tell my husband in my head.

Accept your need for validation. Seek it. Get it. Let it nurture you. Let the voices from the outside drown the judgemental, guilt-ridden inner nag. Take shame for an evening walk with you and leave it behind somewhere on a park bench. Ditch shame. Have an affair with your self-esteem.

It does take a village to raise a child. To raise your inner child. Choose your village.

And please, patience. It takes time to embrace a new village, and for it to embrace you. It takes skill. Put the people you find to good use. Tap into their potential to support and admire you.

I know you hate compliments. Just because you hate it, doesn't mean you don't want it. Feign acceptance till you get it right. If you've come this far, this is yours to keep. Let it lie around, maybe it will make a good present one day. It might even grow on you, who knows.

Make sure you have a weekend full of lots of nothing.

Acknowledgements

The names are coming to me in pairs. These are the people who have helped to make me possible, and therefore this book possible.

Father Oswald Summerton and Dr Pearl Drego—my therapists and teachers—who offered me their wisdom and grace and showed me the way to break free from fear. From Pearl I learnt to separate my self from everything else it gets intertwined in. Her distilled, multi-purpose one-liners have guided me through the years, teaching me to fortify my own boundaries. Father Os taught me to extend myself with generosity and without fear. I keep their teachings close to my heart and draw from the reservoir whenever I need to refresh my sense of self.

Roger Ebert and Priya Ramani—both of whom I met on Twitter—were my earliest readers and champions. Their worlds were already full, they didn't have to extend themselves to include me, but they did. Ebert retweeted my essays and aphorisms to his huge base of followers, creating a global network of connections and deep friendships that gave me a strong, quiet confidence. As the editor of *Mint Lounge*, Priya offered me a regular column and complete freedom to express myself. She introduced me to my own voice. Both of them read me, loved me and showed me the way to the playground again.

My brothers, Nitish and Manish, who are my strength, my happiness and my laughter.

My parents, who have given me everything many times over. Whatever I know about being strong, patient and generous, I have learnt from them. My parents-in-law, Ammi and Papa, from whom I have learnt acceptance and large-heartedness.

My husband and children who are not a pair but four people. They are my kindergarten and my university. They force meaning into my life in return for me forcing them to wake up or take a bath once in a while. Look at it from a distance and it's a fabulous deal I have wrangled for myself.

My best friends—Anshuman Mahaley, Geet Oberoi, Dawn Storey, Helen Vaid, Rachana Pandey, Aparna Roy, Shefali Bhushan, Madhulika Mathur, Radhika Bordia, Rohit Bhatia, Anu Singh Choudhary, Susmita Choudhuri, Anupama Chandra, Manisha Mudgal, Paromita Vohra, Aneela Babar, Raza Haider—and other misfits, smartasses and human personifications of wabi sabi. Friends are the bonus god gave us when he created life. I have been spectacularly blessed in this department.

My childhood uncle, Ishwar Chandra Sinha. There is no one word for the role he has played in my life. There are many—friend, mentor, inspirator. I invented this word just for him.

Most of all, my lifelong gratitude to Dharini Bhaskar, the editor of this book, who, with the lightest of touch, held my hand as I tentatively tiptoed around the boundaries that I myself had drawn around me. She stood in for me when I failed to show up, stayed loyal to me when I abandoned myself, and heard what I was saying when I wouldn't express what I wanted. With extreme generosity, Dharini has dealt with my fears, celebrated what I have created, seen patterns and meaning in words when I have been overwhelmed and brought a rare love and dedication to this book that I could not have imagined if I had not experienced it. Dharini is the magic touch that has made this book possible. 'You should charge me for the therapy I get from you,' I often message her.

Thank you all for protecting me and my vulnerabilities (and letting me get away with an ungrammatical sentence once in a while).